MW00989403

NEW ORLEANS COOK BOOK

Lena Richard

With an Introduction by
GWEN BRISTOW

Dover Publications, Inc.
New York

Published in Canada by General Publishing Company, Ltd., 30 Lesmill Road, Don Mills, Toronto, Ontario.

Published in the United Kingdom by Constable and Company, Ltd.

This Dover edition, first published in 1985, is an unabridged republication of the work first published by Houghton Mifflin Company, Boston, in 1940.

Manufactured in the United States of America
Dover Publications, Inc., 31 East 2nd Street, Mineola, N.Y. 11501

Library of Congress Cataloging in Publication Data

Richard, Lena.
  New Orleans cook book.

  Reprint. Originally published: Boston : Houghton Mifflin, 1940.
  Includes index.
  1. Cookery, American—Louisiana.   I. Title.   II. Title: New Orleans cookbook.
TX715.R502   1985   641.5   84-18805
ISBN 0-486-24819-4 (pbk.)

PREFACE

This book is the result of many years of formulating and collecting of recipes for dishes which I have prepared for luncheons, dinners, parties, teas, and banquets.

Because of the praise I received for my work as a cateress in the city of New Orleans, and because of the constant and insistent demand for my recipes and menus by the housewives, I was inspired to compile my life's work into book form. In order to do this I opened a cooking school in 1937.

My purpose in opening a cooking school was to teach men and women the art of food preparation and serving in order that they would become capable of preparing and serving food for any occasion and also that they might be in a position to demand higher wages. It was also my aim in formulating the 'New Orleans Cook Book,' to put the culinary art within the reach of every housewife and homemaker.

The secrets of Creole cooking which have been kept for years by the old French chef are herein revealed. To the ordinary homemaker Creole Gumbo, Court Bouillon, Crawfish Bisque, Grillade a la Creole, are no longer dishes prepared in secrecy by French chefs, to be eaten by the rich. These may be prepared by anyone following my simple directions. There is no need to experiment, for I have done the experimenting in my own laboratory-kitchen as well as in my cooking school.

LENA RICHARD

CONTENTS

INTRODUCTION

BY GWEN BRISTOW

New Orleans has three seasons, summer, fog, and February. Not that we mind. For our thick blue summers and our thick silver winters produce the materials from which many generations have wrought our great achievement, the indoor art of good dining. As nearly as any art can be conveyed in words, this book explains New Orleans food.

Lena Richard is a great cook, by which we mean that she is a great creator of joy. Oh yes, we know anybody can be healthfully nourished on bread, eggs, and lettuce. Crayfish bisque and shrimp rémoulade are unnecessary to long life. So are the columns of Athens and the paintings of Florence and the rhythms of Edgar Allan Poe.

This book tells you how you may share the joy of New Orleans dining. I can add nothing to a volume that offers recipes for twenty different hot breads, besides directions for making nine such bread variations as banana fritters and *pain perdu*. What can I give a book that explains watermelon ice cream, gumbo filé, baked plantains, daube glacé?

The arts, they tell us, are fallen on evil days. The world is in a most perplexing state. We know this in New Orleans. But we know, too, that we cannot spend all our time wrinkling our foreheads over the future of civilization when its present still gives us so much to enjoy. Good dining remains, and we expect to go on finding pleasure in our dinners until the last flagstone on Chartres Street has been ground to dust by the feet of pilgrims on their way to the French Market.

For our town is, and always has been, a city of refuge. Here we are less aware of the tumult of the days than of the fact that we live each day only once and should enjoy it before it becomes history. The light of the sunset on Lake Pontchartrain, the fog blowing like yards of muslin down the river, the soft lavender tinge of early morning on the Cabildo — these are all a part of the same spirit that cherishes crayfish bisque. It doesn't last long, but then, neither do we.

APPETIZERS

APPETIZERS AND CANAPES

Appetizers are served as a preliminary to the dinner, that they may whet the appetite.

Canapes usually in the form of sliced bread or toast or crackers covered with minced meat, pastes, etc. All very daintily decorated.

CAVIAR CANAPE

Mix one can of Caviar with one teaspoon of lemon juice season with cayenne or three drops of Worcestershire Sauce. Spread thinly over circular slices of bread or toast. Sprinkle with one tablespoon of finely chopped Shallots or chives.

SARDINE CANAPE

Butter various cuts of thinly sliced bread or toast, designed in the shape of circles, hearts, diamonds, etc. Remove the skin and bones from one can of sardines. Mash the sardines and add one teaspoon of melted butter, a dash of tabasco and Worcestershire Sauce, and a pinch of salt. Spread this paste lightly, on the bread or toast. Garnish with one thin slice of stuffed olives in the center.

BACON AND CHEESE APPETIZERS

Mash one Philadelphia cheese, and add to it two tablespoons of crisply fried chopped bacon. Add dash of tabasco and

[1]

Worcestershire Sauce. Spread thinly over dainty crackers, and sprinkle with two tablespoons of chopped shallots or chives. Serve on a platter attractively decorated with curly parsley.

SARDINE AND EGG CANAPE

Spread pieces of buttered toast with a paste made of hard boiled egg yolks, one can of sardines, and a little lemon juice. Chop egg whites, mix with parsley, sprinkle over top with four tablespoons of grated American cheese and melt lightly under the broiler.

BROWN BREAD CANAPE

Mash one Philadelphia cheese with two tablespoons of finely chopped boiled ham, one tablespoon of chopped olives, a dash of cayenne pepper, a pinch of salt, and three drops of Worcestershire Sauce. Spread over very thin slices of brown bread, roll, and cut in pieces one half inch thick.

PEANUT BUTTER AND BACON APPETIZERS

Spread the contents of a small jar of peanut butter over daintily buttered crackers and sprinkle with six tablespoons of crisply fried chopped bacon. Serve brilliantly hot, on a platter attractively decorated with curly parsley.

FRANKFURTER AND AMERICAN CHEESE APPETIZERS

Grind or chop one half pound of frankfurters. Mix with two tablespoons of mayonnaise, one tablespoon of butter, one half teaspoon of salt, six drops of tabasco, and three drops of Worcestershire sauce. Grate six tablespoons of American cheese. Spread the frankfurter mixture on rounds of toast and sprinkle with the grated cheese. Place under broiler until the cheese melts. Serve brilliantly hot.

COCKTAIL PUFFS

6 tablespoons butter
1 cup boiling water
½ teaspoon salt

4 eggs
1 cup flour

Place water in sauce pan, bring to boiling point, add butter. Stir in quickly the flour sifted with salt. Cook until the mixture forms a mass which clears edge of pan. Remove from fire and beat in eggs, one at a time, blending thoroughly. Place in a pastry bag and drop about one teaspoon at a time on a greased baking sheet. Put in a hot oven (450°) for 10 minutes, then reduce heat to 350° and continue cooking for 25 minutes, or until thoroughly dried out inside. This amount will furnish 30 small puffs. These puffs can be filled with the following mixtures: cream shrimp, chicken or turkey, highly seasoned American or Philadelphia cheese, caviar or anchovy paste.

CHEESE BALLS

1 egg
1 cup grated American cheese
¼ cup cracker meal

1 teaspoon Worcestershire sauce
Few drops Tabasco
Salt and pepper to taste

Mix all ingredients together. Form mixture into small balls. Roll in small amount cracker meal and fry in medium hot deep fat. Drain on absorbent paper, stick a tooth pick in each and serve hot.

SUGGESTIONS FOR COCKTAIL CANAPES

1. Toast Canapes: Caviar, anchovy or pate de fois gras, softened with a small amount of mayonnaise and creamed butter and seasoned to taste. Garnish with either pearl onions, parsley, chopped hard-boiled eggs, pimentos or stuffed olives.

2. Bread Canapes: One boiled shrimp sliced in half lengthwise and placed on moon-shaped bread slice which has been spread with mayonnaise and creamed butter seasoned with Tabasco, Worcestershire sauce and onion juice to taste.

[3]

A slice of hard-boiled egg surrounded by a strip of pimento on a round of bread spread with the seasoned mayonnaise and creamed butter. A thin slice of tomato, salted and garnished with parsley, on a whole wheat bread round spread with seasoned mayonnaise and creamed butter.

3. Cracker Canapes: Chopped bacon mixed with peanut butter.

A slice of hard-boiled egg sprinkled with sharp yellow grated cheese on a cracker, spread with a mixture of mayonnaise and hot dry mustard.

COCKTAILS

Cocktails are prepared of fresh or canned fruits or both and should always contain some tart fruit. All fruits are cut in small pieces and no skin is left on except on cherries or grapes. The juice may be poured over the fruit if served with a spoon; if no liquid is used a fork is preferable.

CHERRY AND CANTALOUPE COCKTAIL

3 cups sweet pitted cherries
3 cups cantaloupe

½ cup orange juice or sherry wine
¼ cup lemon juice

Cut cantaloupe in balls or cubes and chill. Arrange in cocktail glasses with cherries in center. Serve with one tablespoon of orange juice or sherry and lemon juice mixed.

FRUIT COCKTAIL

1 grapefruit
2 slices canned pineapple
½ cup sugar

2 oranges
½ cup strawberries or cherries

Remove pulp from the grapefruit and oranges. Cut strawberries in halves. Cut pineapple in small pieces. Sweeten pineapple juice with sugar, and put 2 tablespoons of this juice over fruit which has been arranged in sherbet glasses. Chopped crystallized ginger sprinkled over the top will add to the cocktail. Place in refrigerator until ready to serve.

WATERMELON COCKTAIL

Cut chilled cantaloupe in halves crosswise then remove seeds. Fill with balls cut from chilled watermelon (using a vegetables cutter for shaping balls); sprinkle with granulated sugar and pour over a wineglass of dry ginger ale.

Attractiveness to the cantaloupe may be had by scalloping the cantaloupe all around. Serve as a first course.

SEAFOOD COCKTAIL

Shrimp, crab or fish should always be cooked before using, and the fish and crab meat should then be flaked. Oysters and clams are served raw. Any cocktail ingredient should be thoroughly chilled before placing in cocktail glass. Pour sauce on just before serving.

COCKTAIL SAUCE

1 teaspoon salt	¼ teaspoon Tabasco sauce
½ teaspoon chopped parsley	1 teaspoon Worcestershire sauce
1 teaspoon melted butter	1 teaspoon horseradish
2 tablespoons vinegar	½ cup catsup
	¼ cup finely cut celery

Mix well together and chill thoroughly before pouring over the cocktails.

AVOCADO OR ALLIGATOR PEAR COCKTAIL

Cut 3 medium avocadoes or alligator pears in cubes. Arrange these in cocktail glasses with small lettuce leaves. Pour 4 tablespoons cocktail sauce in each glass. This amount of avocadoes will serve six people. This can be served as a salad on plates, by omitting one tablespoon of dressing.

AVOCADO COCKTAIL SAUCE

1 cup mayonnaise	1 teaspoon Worcestershire sauce
½ cup tomato ketchup	Tabasco, salt, white pepper to taste
2 tablespoons chili sauce	1 teaspoon lemon juice

Mix all ingredients together and use over avocado, hearts of artichoke or seafood cocktail.

[6]

FISH AND OYSTERS

BAKED TURTLE IN SHELL

3 pounds turtle meat
6 strips of fried, chopped bacon
1 medium size onion (chopped)
1 small green pepper (chopped)
2 pods finely chopped garlic
4 tablespoons flour
¼ cup shortening
3 tablespoons butter
1 sprig thyme

1 bay leaf
1 lemon
1 teaspoon chopped parsley
1 teaspoonful   Worcestershire
   sauce
½ cup sherry
½ cup bread crumbs
4 cups mashed potatoes
Few drops Tabasco
Shell of a 4 pound turtle

Boil turtle shell in water until outer skin begins to separate from the shell. Remove shell from water and peel off all this skin. Boil turtle meat in two quarts water for 30 minutes. Remove from fire and strain saving four cups of the water for a gravy. Remove bone from turtle meat. Melt shortening in a saucepan and add flour, let brown slightly. Add onion and allow to brown. Then add bacon, green pepper, garlic, butter, thyme, bay leaf, parsley, Worcestershire sauce, Tabasco, salt and pepper, turtle meat and the four cups of water left over after boiling meat. Let simmer in covered saucepan for 25 minutes. Add the sliced lemon and allow to cook five more minutes. Remove from stove and add sherry.

Make a border with the mashed potatoes all around edge of the shell to hold the turtle filling. Pour turtle mixture in center, sprinkle same with bread crumbs and run in oven to brown.

SHRIMP FILLING

1 egg yolk	½ teaspoon chopped chives
1 teaspoon lemon juice	½ teaspoon chopped parsley
½ teaspoon Worcestershire Sauce	¾ cup chopped boiled shrimp
½ teaspoon Tabasco	1 cup cream sauce

Add shrimp and all seasonings to hot cream sauce. Beat egg yolk and add last to mixture. Cook for few minutes. Slit each puff on side and fill with cream mixture. Run in oven and serve while hot. This will fill sixty cocktail puffs.

SCALED FISH

3 pounds Red Snapper or Red Fish	1 tablespoon vinegar
14 green olives	3 tablespoons salt
14 ripe olives	1½ quarts water
1 small can pimentos	1 onion
2 tablespoons gelatine	1 bay leaf
1 teaspoon Worcestershire sauce	1 sprig thyme
½ teaspoon Tabasco sauce	1 small piece of celery
	½ lemon

Fish mold is necessary for this recipe.

Boil fish for 10 minutes in water seasoned with all above seasonings. Remove fish from water and set aside. Strain fish stock. Soak gelatine in ¼ cup cold water then dissolve sauce in 2 cups hot fish stock. Slice all olives to fit scale depressions of mold. Line mold scales with alternate green and ripe slices of olives. Follow design of fish tail and fin with thin strips of pimento and in like manner use pimento to mark gill and mouth. Around eyes, curve small strip of pimento, inside of which place a small piece of black olive for eye ball.

Flake fish and fill mold until ¾ full. Pour gelatine mixture over all, cover and place in refrigerator to congeal. Serve on bed of lettuce with Hollandaise Sauce or Remoulade Sauce. Any other firm-meated fish may be used.

CRAB MOUSSE

2 cups crab meat
¾ cup cracker crumbs
4 eggs
1 cup milk
¼ cup butter
¼ teaspoon finely chopped garlic
1 teaspoon Worcestershire sauce

1 tablespoon finely chopped onion
1 tablespoon finely chopped parsley or chives
Few drops Tabasco
2 teaspoons baking powder
Salt and pepper to taste

Mix all above ingredients together in order given and stir well. Grease a ring mold with butter and pour crab mixture in mold. Place mold in or over a large pot of boiling water. Allow to simmer slowly for 45 minutes. When ready to serve, remove mousse from mold by reversing on platter. Fish can be substituted in the same method.

SEAFOOD SAUCE

3 cups medium cream sauce
½ cup crab meat
1 cup boiled and cut shrimp
2 tablespoons chopped onion
½ teaspoon finely chopped garlic
1 tablespoon chopped green pepper

2 tablespoons lemon juice
1 teaspoon Worcestershire sauce
1 teaspoon paprika
1 tablespoon chopped celery
1 tablespoon chopped parsley
3 tablespoons sherry
Salt and pepper to taste

Mix all ingredients except sherry in order named. Cook for five minutes. Then remove from fire and add sherry.

Use this sauce to fill the center and pour over the crab mousse.

TUNA AND POTATO SOUFFLE

1 lb. can tuna (2 cups)
2 tablespoons butter
2 tablespoons chopped celery
2 tablespoons chopped parsley
2 cups seasoned mashed potatoes

3 eggs
1 teaspoon salt
1 teaspoon minced onion
1 tablespoon lemon juice
Few drops Tabasco sauce

Drain the tuna, flake it with a fork. Melt the fat and cook the celery and parsley in it for a few minutes. Then combine

[9]

with the tuna, mashed potatoes, and seasonings; add the beaten egg yolks, and beat the mixture until very light. Fold in the well beaten whites of eggs, pile lightly, at once into a greased baking pan, and bake in a moderate oven (350°) for 1 hour, or until set in the center and lightly browned. Serve in the dish. Salmon Souffle can be made in the same order.

BAKED STUFFED OYSTERS

6 large or 8 small oysters shells are used in this recipe, but, if these are not available, any other individual baking dish may be used.

2 dozen large oysters or 3 dozen small
2 cups oyster liquor
2 small onions
1 clove garlic
1 green pepper
1 small piece celery
2 teaspoons lemon juice

2 dashes Tabasco sauce
1 teaspoon paprika
½ teaspoon Worcestershire Sauce
½ cup cooking oil
4 tablespoons butter
½ cup mushrooms
1¼ cup bread crumbs
⅓ cup flour

Drain oysters and chop into coarse pieces. Chop onion, garlic, green pepper and celery. Make a roux in frying pan with oil and flour. Let brown then add onion, garlic, celery and green pepper and cook slowly until seasonings are browned. Then add to this mixture the oysters, chopped mushrooms, oyster water and all other ingredients, except bread crumbs. Cook for ten minutes. Set aside 2 tablespoons of the mixture to use as a sauce for each oyster. To the remainder add 1 cup bread crumbs, stir and remove from fire. Fill oyster shells with oyster mixture, sprinkle with ¼ cup bread crumbs and bake in a moderate oven fifteen minutes. Remove stuffed shells from oven and place on plates. Heat sauce and pour over stuffed oysters.

COURT BOUILLON

1 pound sliced red snapper or red fish	1 sprig thyme
	1 bay leaf
1 cup canned tomatoes	½ lemon
1 medium sized onion (chopped)	½ cup shortening
1 tablespoon chopped green pepper	4 tablespoons flour
	1 cup water
¼ teaspoon chopped garlic	Salt and pepper to taste

Make a roux with the shortening, flour and onion, add the rest of the ingredients except fish and cook ten minutes. Add the sliced fish and let cook on slow fire for 15 minutes. Court-bouillon may be served on toast and with mashed potatoes or rice. This recipe will serve four people.

SHRIMP FRICASSEE A LA CREOLE

2 pounds of large shrimp	1 tablespoon chopped green pepper
1 cup canned tomatoes	
2 tablespoons chopped onions	1 tablespoon chopped celery
¼ teaspoon chopped garlic	4 tablespoons flour
1 sprig thyme	2 cups water
2 sprigs parsley	4 tablespoons shortening
1 bay leaf	Salt and pepper to taste

Peel shrimp, remove black vein and wash well. Make a roux with shortening, flour and onions. Add tomatoes and water, shrimp and all seasonings. Simmer 20 minutes. This dish can be served very attractively in a mold of rice.

CRAB FRICASSEE

1 dozen hard shelled crabs	1 bay leaf
1 medium sized onion (chopped)	½ cup shortening
1 tablespoon chopped green pepper	4 tablespoons flour
	2 cups water
¼ teaspoon chopped garlic	Salt and pepper to taste
1 sprig thyme	

Scald crabs with boiling water. Remove the top shells. Remove the "dead man's fingers" and take off the spongy substance. Break crabs into halves. Make a roux with shortening, flour and onion. When browned add water, crabs and other ingredients. Cook 20 minutes. Serve with rice. See page 135 for making of Roux.

CODFISH BALLS

2½ cups mashed potatoes	¼ teaspoon chopped parsley
1 cup codfish flakes	½ tablespoon chopped onion
1 egg	½ teaspoon pepper
1 teaspoon butter	Salt to taste

To potatoes, add butter, beaten egg, seasonings and codfish. Shape into round balls or croquettes and leave in ice box until ready to cook. Fry in deep fat until brown.

SEAFOOD AND ASPARAGUS VOL-AU-VENT

4 lbs. Red Snapper or Red Fish	2 tablespoons salt
1 quart of water	1 teaspoon white or black pepper
1 sprig thyme	1 small onion
1 sprig celery	1 bay leaf

Bring water with seasonings to boiling point and in this boil fish 20 minutes. Turn once while boiling. Remove fish from water, drain, skin and when cool remove all bones. Set fish on back of stove to keep hot until sauce has been prepared.

SAUCE

1 pound shrimp *or*	¼ pound butter
3 pounds crayfish	½ cup chopped pimentoes
1 No. 2 can asparagus tips	¼ cup celery
1 cup mushrooms	¼ cup sherry
2 egg yolks	Juice ½ lemon
3 tablespoons flour	1 teaspoon Worcestershire sauce
1 cup milk	A few drops Tabasco or cay-
½ cup cream	enne pepper. White pepper
½ cup fish liquor	and salt to taste

Peel raw shrimp or crawfish and remove black vein careful-ly. Blend flour in melted butter, add mushrooms, shrimp or crawfish, then add milk, cream and fish liquor, chopped pi-mentoes. Cook 15 minutes. Just before pouring sauce over

fish, add well-beaten egg yolks, lemon juice, sherry and seasonings. Cook 5 minutes longer.

TO SERVE

Place fish broken into pieces in bottom of vol-au-vent, alternate with asparagus tips, which have been drained. Over this
pour the sauce and garnish with parsley. If crayfish have been
used, a few whole cooked crayfish will add to the decoration
of this dish.

STUFFED OR DEVILED CRABS

(If crab shells are not available, any other individual baking
dishes may be used.)

1 dozen crabs	1 small piece celery (chopped)
1 cup bread crumbs	½ green pepper (chopped)
1 medium-size onion (chopped)	½ pod garlic (chopped)
1 hard-boiled egg (chopped	2 raw eggs
½ cup sweet cream	2 tablespoons chopped parsley
2 tablespoons butter	Salt and pepper to taste
1 tablespoon cooking oil	1 tablespoon vinegar
1 sprig thyme	

Boil crabs for 15 minutes, drain, let cool and remove meat.
Mix thoroughly together all ingredients. Cook for 10 minutes
in melted butter and oil. Stuff well-washed crab shells. Sprinkle
over bread crumbs and place in oven to brown. Serve with
Lemon and Butter Sauce.

BROILED FISH

Split or tenderloin fish. Wash, drain and season with pepper
and salt to taste. Brush thoroughly with cooking oil and place
under hot flame. Let broil quickly for 15 to 20 minutes. When
cooked remove from fire and allow fish to stand in covered
dish several minutes before serving. Serve with Hot lemon and
Butter Sauce, (page 69) garnished with slices of lemon and
chopped parsley.

CREAMED SHRIMP

1 cup raw peeled shrimp
3 tablespoons butter
2 tablespoons flour
1 cup hot milk
¼ cup cream

1 teaspoon lemon juice
1 tablespoon chopped parsley
¼ teaspoon Worcestershire sauce
Cayenne, salt and pepper to taste

Melt butter, add flour. Pour in hot milk slowly, stirring to prevent lumping. Add shrimp and the rest of seasonings. Let cook for 20 minutes over a double boiler. Just before serving add parsley and serve.

TUNA A LA KING

1 cup Tuna fish
3 tablespoons finely chopped pimento
3 tablespoons butter
2 tablespoons flour
1 tablespoon lemon juice

1 egg yolk
1 cup hot milk
½ teaspoon Coleman's dry mustard
Salt and pepper to taste

Melt butter, add flour and milk slowly. Add tuna fish and pimento. Add rest of seasonings. Remove from fire. Just before ready to serve, add well beaten yolk of egg. Let cook for 3 to 5 minutes. Two tablespoons of sherry may be added if desired.

Tuna a la King can be served in Potato Baskets, in Timbales or on toast.

CRAB A LA KING

½ pound crabmeat
½ cup mushroom
3 tablespoons green pepper
3 tablespoons pimento
1 cup light cream
1 cup milk
4 tablespoons flour

2 tablespoons lemon juice
6 tablespoons butter
2 egg yolks
1 teaspoon Coleman's dry mustard
Salt and pepper to taste

Melt butter, add flour then milk slowly. Add crabmeat, pimento and mushroom. Add rest of reasonings and cream. Let cook 5 minutes. Remove from fire. Just before ready to serve add well beaten yolks of eggs and lemon juice. Let cook for 3 to 5 minutes. Two tablespoons of sherry may be added if desired. Crab a la King can be served in Potato Baskets, in Timbales or on toast. Shrimp, chicken or crayfish may be substituted for crabmeat.

OYSTER POULET

3 dozen oysters
1 cup boiled and peeled shrimp
3 tablespoons cooking oil
4 tablespoons butter
1 cup milk
1 cup oyster water
2 tablespoons chopped onion
¼ teaspoon finely chopped garlic

1 tablespoon chopped green pepper
3 egg yolks
4 tablespoons flour (heaping)
3 tablespoons lemon juice
1 teaspoon Worcestershire sauce
1 teaspoon paprika
Salt and pepper to taste

Place oil and butter in a sauce pan to melt, then add flour, oysters and all other ingredients except eggs. Cook on a slow fire about 15 minutes until thickened. Just before serving beat egg yolks, stir into the mixture and cook a few minutes longer. This may be served in any kind of pastry shells.

FRIED TENDERLOINED FISH

Wash slices of fish, drain and season well with salt and pepper. Dip into egg wash, dredge in cornmeal and fry in hot fat for three to five minutes. If slices are larger than usual, cook longer until well browned.

CRAB CUTLETS

2 cups crab meat
1¾ cups cracker meal
2 eggs
½ cup milk
Dash of cayenne pepper

3 tablespoons chopped onion
2 tablespoons parsley
1 chopped green pepper
1 teaspoon salt

Chop crab meat. Add seasoning. Mix well, then add whole eggs, milk and one cup of the cracker meal. Mold, insert crab

[15]

claw into croquette. Roll in ¾ cup cracker meal. Allow to chill in refrigerator at least one hour. Just before serving, fry in deep fat until a golden brown. May be served as a first or the main course of a dinner.

Use Lena's Red Sauce (see page 70), for crab cutlets.

OYSTERS A LA ROCKEFELLER

3 dozens large oysters on the half shell
4 tablespoons finely chopped onion
1 teaspoon finely chopped garlic
4 tablespoons finely chopped green pepper
2 tablespoons finely chopped celery
Juice of 2 lemons

1 tablespoon Worcestershire sauce
2 tablespoons chili
¾ pound butter
¾ cup bread crumbs
1½ cups water
4 teaspoons chopped bacon
Salt, white pepper and cayenne pepper to taste

Mix all ingredients, except butter, thoroughly. Melt butter in a sauce pan, add the first mixture to melted butter and let cook five minutes. Arrange a bed of rock salt in a tin pan; place six oysters on the bed of salt, and over each oyster put one heaping tablespoon of the cooked dressing and bake in hot oven for 10 minutes. On each oyster serve 1 tablespoon of Rockefeller Cream Green Sauce.

RECEIPT FOR GREEN SAUCE

2 cups boiled spinach
2 tablespoons flour
¼ pound butter
2 tablespoons vinegar
¾ cup water

2 dashes of Tabasco Sauce
4 drops Absinthe
4 tablespoons finely chopped parsley
1 teaspoon salt

Pass the boiled spinach through a sieve. Melt butter, add flour, spinach, water and seasoning. Let cook for three minutes and serve. This recipe will serve six.

OYSTERS EN BROCHETTE

Select large oysters. Alternate four oysters with four squares of bacon on a skewer. Broil under flame until bacon browns. Serve on toast. Make a sauce by adding 2 tablespoons butter, 1 teaspoon lemon juice and 1 tablespoon chopped parsley to the oyster and bacon drippings. Pour over each portion of oyster brochette.

SOUPS AND GUMBO

—❖❀❖—

SHRIMP BISQUE

3 pounds large lake shrimp
¼ cup shortening or bacon fat
5 tablespoons flour
3 tablespoons chopped onions
1 cup canned tomatoes
1 tablespoon chopped green pepper
½ teaspoon chopped garlic
1 sprig thyme
1 bay leaf
3 tablespoons chopped parsley
½ teaspoon cayenne
¼ teaspoon white pepper
6 tablespoons cracker or bread crumbs
4 tablespoons butter
1 teaspoon onion juice
Salt to taste

Wash thoroughly and peel and remove heads of raw shrimp. Remove veins. Scoop out heads and set aside, keeping scrapings to cook. Put shells and scrapings from heads on to cook in two quarts cold water. Let cook to a boil. Remove and strain. Prepare roux with shortening or bacon fat and flour letting flour brown first then adding onions to brown. Add tomatoes, let cook a few minutes then add stock, all seasonings and half the amount shrimp cut in small pieces. Let simmer for about one hour.

Chop fine the remainder of shrimp, add cracker crumbs, eggs beaten with 3 tablespoons water, onion juice, salt and pepper to taste. Fry mixture in butter for 5 minutes. Stuff heads, place on pan, sprinkle with crumbs, place in hot oven to brown.

Let heads cook in soup for five minutes before serving. If any dressing is left over from the stuffing of the heads, it may be added to the soup.

[18]

CRAWFISH BISQUE

5 pounds crawfish	4 tablespoons chopped parsley
1 large onion	1 cup fine bread crumbs
2 pods garlic	4 tablespoons butter
2 bay leaves	½ cup shortening
1 sprig thyme	2 eggs
1 green pepper	3 quarts water
1 tablespoon finely chopped	¾ cup flour
celery	Salt and pepper to taste

Boil and pick crawfish. Clean 24 crawfish heads, leaving only the shells. Boil entire remainder of crawfish in 3 quarts of water for 5 minutes. Remove from fire and strain. Set crawfish stock aside.

Chop crawfish meat, add all seasonings and mix with eggs and bread crumbs. Add to this a small amount of the crawfish water, only enough to soften the mixture. Fry this in butter for 5 minutes and stuff crawfish heads with same.

Make a "roux" (see page 135) with the shortening and flour, then add remainder of crawfish water and let cook on slow fire 40 minutes. Place stuffed heads in oven and brown slightly. Then cook in soup 5 minutes before serving. Allow four to six heads per person.

TURTLE SOUP

2 pounds turtle meat	½ cup flour
2 bay leaves	1 No. 2 can tomatoes
1 green pepper	2 pods garlic
1 lemon	6 cloves
½ cup cooking oil	4 tablespoons butter
1 wine glass sherry	1 large onion
1 small slice raw ham	5 eggs
1 sprig thyme	Salt, cayenne and pepper to
½ teaspoon ground all spice	taste
1 tablespoon Worcestershire	
sauce	

Boil turtle meat in one gallon water until tender. Strain and set water aside. Make a roux with oil, flour and onion, then add tomatoes and let simmer for 5 minutes. Mince turtle meat and ham, add to strained turtle water then the roux, except sherry, eggs and lemon. Boil slowly for 55 minutes. Add whole lemon squeezed and balance of seasonings. Let cook 5 minutes longer. Pour sherry in and serve in plates or cups, with slices of lemon and finely chopped hard boiled eggs.

CREAM OF SALMON SOUP

1 can salmon
1 quart milk
5 tablespoons butter

1 tablespoon flour
Salt and pepper to taste

Scald the milk in a double boiler, then stir in the salmon and salmon liquor. Pass through a sieve, pressing it until the juice is extracted and the salmon is dry. Melt butter, add flour, blend well and add first mixture. Cook in double boiler. The soup is ready to serve when it is of a creamy consistency. Pour into cups and garnish with whipped cream, chopped parsley or paprika.

RED BEAN PUREE

2 cups red beans
1 medium onion
½ pound pickled meat *or* ham
  shank
¼ teaspoon finely chopped garlic
1 sprig thyme

2 bay leaves
4 hard-boiled eggs
1 lemon
3 quarts water
½ cup sherry
3 tablespoons butter

Soak red beans over night in 1 quart of water. Boil red beans, meat and seasonings together with remainder of water. Let boil until water has reduced to 1 quart. Then strain and rub beans through a sieve. Season with salt and pepper to taste. Add butter and cook a few minutes longer. Just before serving, pour in sherry, add finely chopped eggs and slices of lemon.

CLEAR CORN SOUP

2 cups corn canned *or*
2 cups fresh corn
6 slices crisply fried bacon
1 tablespoon chopped onion

1 pint milk
1 cup canned tomatoes
Salt and pepper to taste
Pinch cooking soda

Boil all ingredients, except bacon, for 5 minutes. Remove from fire. Rub through sieve then add bacon. Just before serving, heat. Serve in soup cups topped with whipped cream and chopped parsley.

CREAM OF CORN SOUP

2 cups corn (canned or fresh)	3 tablespoons flour
2 cups water	4 tablespoons butter
2 cups milk	1 teaspoon onion juice

Let corn and water cook for 20 minutes then strain. Melt butter and flour, stir until well blended. Then pour the hot milk stirring continually. Add strained corn and water, onion juice. Season with salt and pepper to taste.

SPLIT PEA SOUP

2 cups dried split peas	2 tablespoons baking dripping
1 slice salted pork	3 quarts water
2 tablespoons chopped onion	

Soak peas in 1 quart of water overnight. Cook with 2 quarts water, onion, bacon dripping and salted pork. Cook until tender. Pass through sieve. Season with salt and pepper to taste. Serve piping hot with toast or crackers. Sherry can be added if desired.

CREAM OF CRAB SOUP

2 cups crab meat	1 teaspoon finely chopped onion
6 cups milk	1 tablespoon finely chopped
4 tablespoons flour	celery
4 tablespoons butter	

Melt butter, stirring flour, onion and celery until it all blends well. Add Scalded milk, crab meat. Season with salt, pepper and tabasco sauce to taste. Let cook over double boiler for 15 or 20 minutes. Top with whipped cream and chopped parsley and serve.

OKRA GUMBO

2 pounds okra (finely cut)
6 crabs
1 pound shrimps
1 medium slice raw ham
1½ cups canned tomatoes
½ cup shortening
4 tablespoons chopped onion
2 tablespoons chopped green pepper

2 pods garlic
2 tablespoons flour
2 quarts water
2 bay leaves
1 sprig thyme
1 tablespoon chopped celery
Cayenne pepper and salt to suit taste

Make a roux (see page 135) with shortening and onion. Add okra, let fry until brown and dry. Stir to prevent from burning. Then add all the ingredients and hot water and let simmer for 1 hour. It is a custom to serve Okra Gumbo with boiled dry rice.

OX-TAIL SOUP

1 small piece celery
3 pounds ox-tail
4 quarts water
1 tablespoon lard
1 tablespoon flour
1 slice ham
3 tablespoons barley

1 large onion
2 carrots
3 cloves
1 sprig thyme
2 sprigs parsley (chopped)
Salt and pepper to taste

Cut ox-tail into inch cubes. Brown chopped onion and ox-tail in frying pan. Cut ham and carrots into pieces about an inch in size; add this to the meat, stir and add flour to brown. Continue stirring and when browned add the boiling water and seasonings. Lastly add the barley and simmer for four hours. Serve with crackers or curly toast.

BEEF TEA

Cut two pounds of lean beef into half inch cubes and place in covered glass fruit jar. Let stand in pan of hot water for about 3 hours, or until meat loses red color. Pour juice from meat.

This broth will keep on ice for 12 to 24 hours. It needs little seasoning and should be served hot.

BOUILLON

4 pounds beef cut from rump, shin or leg	2 sprigs of thyme
4 bay leaves	2 lemons
1 large onion	3 egg whites
Few pieces celery top	Shells of 3 eggs
	Salt and pepper to taste

Boil the meat in about 1½ gallons of hot water with all the seasoning except the eggshells, egg whites (unbeaten), salt and pepper and the lemons. Boil approximately four hours. When the meat is tender let it stand overnight or at least six or eight hours. Skim all the scum and fat off the top of the meat stock and put back on the fire to heat adding three or four sprigs of parsley, the lemons cut in half and squeezed, (add juice and rind) eggshells, and unbeaten egg whites. Stir constantly until the soup begins to boil, to prevent the egg whites from settling in the bottom of the pot. Boil hard from 3 to 5 minutes. Remove from fire and strain in a clean cloth just thick enough to keep in the scum, only letting the clear soup drip through. Cheese cloth is unsuitable for this. Season with salt and pepper and sherry if desired. Serve with a slice of lemon in each cup.

The jelly Bouillon can be made by this same method using veal instead of beef, two calf feet or four tablespoons of gelatine.

Four tablespoons of Kitchen Bouquet or Caramel Coloring (Page 135) may be added to darken the Bouillon.

GUMBO FILE

1 cup chopped chicken meat	3 teaspoons filé
2½ quarts chicken stock	1 medium sized onion
½ dozen crabs	1 clove of garlic
1 pound lake shrimp	3 tablespoons flour
½ pound or 1 slice raw ham	4 tablespoons cooking oil
1 bay leaf	Salt and pepper to taste

Fry ham and shrimp in cooking oil until ham is a golden brown. Remove ham and shrimp from fat. Make a roux with flour and fat, add onions and cook until a golden brown. Add crabs, chicken, ham and shrimp, stock and all seasonings except salt and pepper. Cook over a slow fire until liquid has reduced to about 1½ quarts. Season with salt and pepper and, just before serving, stir in file. It is customary to serve Gumbo File with rice.

OYSTER CHOWDER

4 dozen oysters
2 tablespoons chopped onions
½ cup crisply fried bacon (chopped)
2 tablespoons chopped celery
1 teaspoon Worcestershire sauce
2 teaspoons lemon juice
4 tablespoons flour
¼ pound butter
8 cups water

Cook oysters in water until boiling point is reached. Skim and cook 3 minutes longer. Remove from fire and strain. Save water. Chop oysters into very small pieces, then add chopped oysters, bacon and all other seasonings to water in which oysters had been cooked. Make a roux of butter, flour and onion. Pour small amount of oyster soup slowly into roux. Blend carefully and combine with remainder of soup. Cook for fifteen or twenty minutes. Serve in cups with dash of whipped cream.

BREAD AND BISCUITS

BAKING POWDER BISCUITS

2 cups flour
4 teaspoons baking powder
½ teaspoon salt

5 tablespoons shortening
2/3 cup milk

Sift flour and measure. Mix flour, baking powder and salt. Cut in fat with a knife or finger tips. Slowly add milk until a soft dough has formed. Pat out on floured board until the dough is ¼ of an inch thick. Cut with biscuit cutter. Bake in 400° oven 12 minutes.

LENA'S CORN BREAD

1 cup corn meal
1½ cups milk
1 cup flour
2 eggs
2 tablespoons sugar

4 teaspoons baking powder
1 teaspoon salt
2 tablespoons cooking oil
2 tablespoons melted butter

Sift together dry ingredients. Beat eggs and mix with milk. Add dry ingredients to eggs and milk mixture, then the oil and melted butter and bake in a pan for 20 to 25 minutes in a moderate oven (350°F.).

ORANGE BREAD

3 cups sifted flour
3 teaspoons baking powder
Rind of 1 large or 2 small oranges
1½ cups sugar

1 cup milk
3 tablespoons butter
1 egg
1 teaspoon salt

Peel oranges and pass rind through grinder. Place in saucepan and cover with water. Boil until peel is tender. To this add milk, sugar and butter. Cook until a thick syrup forms. Remove and cool. Beat egg until light and add to syrup. Sift dry ingredients together. Pour syrup slowly into flour and stir until well blended. Pour mixture on thickly floured board and work flour in until easily handled. Form two small loaves. Bake in 350° oven for 45 minutes. Remove from oven, brush with butter and serve hot or cold.

SPOON BREAD

3 cups milk	6 tablespoons sugar
4 eggs	1 teaspoon salt
1 cup sifted corn meal	½ cup butter
1 cup sifted flour	2 teaspoons baking powder

Separate egg yolks from whites. Beat, then add sugar, butter and salt. Cream until light. Sift dry ingredients, add alternately with milk to the first mixture. Fold in stiffly beaten whites of eggs. Pour into well-greased pyrex dish and bake in 350° oven for 50 minutes.

HOMEMADE BREAD

2 tablespoons sugar	1 cake yeast
2 tablespoons lard or butter	7 cups flour
2 cups scalded milk	2 teaspoons salt

Mix yeast, salt, sugar and shortening in a bowl and then add the lukewarm milk. Stir in the sifted flour until a stiff dough forms. Turn out on a well-floured board and knead until dough is smooth. Brush over lightly with melted butter, cover and set aside to rise in a warm place. When the dough is twice its first size, turn out on a floured board and divide into at least three parts. Shape into loaves and put in a buttered pan. Cover and set to rise. When light, bake in a 350° oven for 40 or 50 minutes.

AFTERNOON TEA BISCUITS

3 cups sifted flour
3 teaspoons baking powder
2/3 cup milk

1/3 teaspoon salt
1/3 cup butter or shortening

Sift flour once, measure, add baking powder and salt, and sift and measure again. Cut in shortening. Add milk gradually until soft dough is formed. Turn on floured board, knead slightly, roll ¾ inch thick, and cut with small floured biscuit cutter. Bake in hot oven 12 to 15 minutes.

ORANGE BISCUITS

2 cups sifted flour
2 teaspoons baking powder
½ teaspoon salt
2 tablespoons sugar
¼ cup orange juice

4 tablespoons butter or shortening
1 tablespoon grated orange rind
2/3 cup milk
12 cubes sugar

Sift flour once, measure, add baking powder, salt, and sugar, and sift again. Cut in shortening and orange rind. Add milk gradually until soft dough is formed. Roll ½ inch thick on slightly floured board. Cut with small biscuit cutter. On top of each biscuit place ½ cube of sugar dipped in orange juice. Bake in hot oven 15 minutes.

CHEESE BISCUITS

1 cup sifted flour
1 teaspoon baking powder
½ cup grated American Cheese
½ teaspoon salt

1 tablespoon butter or shortening
⅜ cup milk or water

Sift flour once, measure, add baking powder and salt, and sift again. Cut in shortening and cheese, add liquid gradually until soft dough is formed. Roll 1/3 inch thick on slightly floured board. Cut with small biscuit cutter. Bake in hot 450° oven 15 minutes.

PAIN PERDU

12 slices of stale bread
3 whole eggs
½ cup sugar

1 cup milk
1 teaspoon of vanilla, cinnamon
or nutmeg

Beat eggs until light and add sugar, flavoring and milk, beat again. Dip slices of bread in mixture and fry in hot deep fat until brown. Serve hot.

CALAS TOUS CHAUDS

2 cups cooked rice
1 Fleischman yeast cake
4 cups flour

2 eggs
4 tablespoons sugar
1½ teaspoons salt

Dissolve yeast in one-half cup lukewarm water. Stir into rice. Let rise overnight. Beat eggs until light, add salt and sugar, combine with rice mixture and stir in flour. Let rise for one hour. Drop by tablespoonful into deep medium hot fat and fry until browned. Drain and serve piping hot with cane syrup. Or, if preferred, sprinkle with powdered sugar and serve hot.

CORN STICKS

1 cup corn meal
1¼ cups milk
¾ cup flour
2 eggs
¼ cup molasses

4 teaspoons baking powder
1 teaspoon salt
2 tablespoons cooking oil
2 tablespoons butter

Sift together flour, salt and baking powder. Pour scalded milk over corn meal and mix thoroughly. Let cool until lukewarm then add molasses and well beaten eggs. Lastly add cooking oil and melted butter. Pour mixture into greased bread stick pan and bake in hot oven for 20 minutes.

IRISH POTATO ROLLS

1 cup milk
2 baked or boiled potatoes
1 tablespoon butter
2 cups flour

1 teaspoon salt
1 egg
½ Fleischman yeast cake

Skin two freshly baked (or boiled) potatoes and put through a ricer. Dissolve yeast cake in lukewarm milk. Add to this beaten egg, salt and melted butter then add flour and potatoes and beat until light. Let rise for about two hours. Use just enough flour to handle lightly on board and knead well and replace in greased pan to rise double in bulk. Roll to one-half inch thickness. Cut with biscuit cutter, place in greased pan. Allow to rise until bulk is doubled, then bake in 450° oven for 15 to 20 minutes. Brush with melted butter just before removing from oven.

CREAM WAFFLES

½ cup cooking oil	3 cups flour
1½ cups milk	4 tablespoons sugar
3 teaspoons baking powder	1 teaspoon salt
2 eggs	

Mix and sift dry ingredients. Beat into the egg yolks first the oil, and then the milk. Combine the two mixtures and beat until smooth. Fold in well beaten egg whites. Pour ¾ cup batter on hot waffle iron. Bake 3 to 4 minutes.

NUT WAFFLES

1¾ cups flour	¾ cup chopped nuts
3 teaspoons baking powder	¼ cup cooking oil
1 tablespoon sugar	1 cup milk
1 teaspoon salt	2 eggs

Mix and sift the dry ingredients. Beat oil into the egg yolks and then the milk. Combine the two mixtures and beat until smooth. Fold in chopped pecans and beaten egg whites. Pour ¾ cup of batter on hot waffle iron. Bake 3 to 4 minutes.

CHOCOLATE WAFFLES

½ cup cooking oil	4 tablespoons sugar
2 squares melted chocolate	3 teaspoons baking powder
1 teaspoon vanilla	1 teaspoon salt
3 cups flour	1½ cups milk
2 eggs	

Sift flour, sugar, salt and baking powder togther. Beat egg yolks and add to milk. Combine mixtures, add cooking oil, vanilla and melted chocolate. Fold in beaten egg whites last. Pour ¾ cup of batter on hot waffle iron. Bake 3 to 4 minutes. Serve plain or with ice cream.

BUTTER ROLLS

3 eggs	4 tablespoons sugar
2 yeast cakes	1 teaspoon salt
6 tablespoons butter	2 cups milk
8 cups flour (approximately)	

Mash and mix together in a bowl the yeast. Add sugar, salt and eggs. Heat milk luke warm. Add butter to the milk, then add to first mixture. Add seven cups of flour, mix well. Put remainder of flour on board. Knead until pastry blisters then set aside to rise for 1½ hours in a warm place. Roll out on floured board, ½ inch thick, brush with melted butter and cut with biscuit cutter. Fold each roll into pocket-book shape and let rise for another 1½ hours. Then bake in hot 450° oven about 15 minutes.

CLOVER LEAF ROLLS

Using Butter Roll Recipe, break dough into small pieces about size of marbles. Brush with fat and place 3 or 4 of these tiny balls close together in greased muffin rings or pans. When very light bake about 15 minutes in hot oven (400°-425°). The success of these rolls depends on having the 3 balls together equal only as much dough as an ordinary roll would require, and letting them rise very light before baking them.

CORN FRITTERS

1½ cups cold water	3 cups flour
1 cup canned corn *or*	4 teaspoons baking powder
1 cup finely cut fresh corn	4 tablespoons sugar
2 eggs	1 teaspoon salt

Beat eggs, sugar and salt, add the water, corn, flour and baking powder. Beat a few minutes. Drop by spoonsful into deep hot fat. Drain on absorbent paper, and serve hot.

PINEAPPLE FRITTERS

8 slices pineapple
1 cup sifted flour
2 eggs
6 tablespoons sugar

¼ teaspoon salt
2 teaspoons baking powder
¾ cups water
Powdered sugar

Cut slices in half and sprinkle with 4 tablespoons sugar. Beat egg yolks until light, add 2 tablespoons sugar and salt. Beat into this mixture alternately the flour, baking powder and water. Fold in well beaten egg whites. Dip pineapple into batter and fry until brown in deep fat. Dust with powdered sugar, if desired.

Pineapple fritters may be served with meats, game or fowl.

BANANA FRITTERS

3 bananas
2 tablespoons sugar
2 eggs
1½ cups flour

¼ teaspoon salt
2/3 cup cold water
2 teaspoons baking powder

Sift dry ingredients. Separate eggs, beat yolks until light then alternate dry ingredients with water. Beat egg whites stiff and fold into first mixture. Peel bananas, cut in half, then lengthwise. Put a few pieces, at a time, in the batter. Dip by spoonfuls the size of the bananas and fry in deep fat. When brown and cooked through, put on absorbent paper. Sprinkle with powdered sugar and serve.

CHEESE STICKS

½ cup grated cheese
½ cup shortening
1½ cups flour

½ teaspoon salt
½ teaspoon cayenne pepper
¼ cup cold water

Mix flour with shortening, either with tips of fingers or cutting in with knife. Stir in salt, pepper, cheese and cold water. Roll on floured board and cut into sticks about 4 inches long. Bake in hot oven until dry. Serve with salads or cocktails.

CURLY TOAST

Have fresh bread sliced very thin (No. 6 on slicing machine). Remove crust, spread with thick coating of butter. Fold diagonally. Then twist bread in a roll and hold together with toothpicks. Toast all over; remove toothpicks and serve immediately.

TOAST CASES

Cut stale bread in 2½ inch cubes. Trim off all crust and hollow out center, leaving sides of box half an inch thick. Toast in a hot oven until delicately browned but not dried; remove from oven and butter. Fill cases with creamed vegetables, creamed eggs, creamed meats, chicken a la king, sweetbreads or a relish of sardine, anchovy, eggs and capers. This may be served as a first course for a dinner or luncheon.

CINNAMON TOAST

6 slices bread	½ cup confectioner's sugar
3 tablespoons butter	1 tablespoon cinnamon

Have bread sliced No. 8 on slicing machine or medium by hand. Remove crust, cut slice in half and toast on one side. Cream butter, sugar and cinnamon; spread thickly on untoasted side of bread. Return to oven and toast slowly until mixture melts. Serve immediately.

Ordinary toast is cooked in the broiler. Cut to thickness desired according to use.

FRENCH TOAST

Follow recipe for Pain Perdu except for one difference. Do not add sugar to mixture in which bread is to be dipped. Simply dip bread into flavored egg and milk mixture, fry in hot deep fat. Serve with syrup or sprinkled over with powdered sugar.

MELBA TOAST

Have bread sliced very thin. Dry in top of very slow oven. May be served dry or with butter.

TIMBALES

1 cup flour	2 tablespoons sugar
¾ cup water	½ teaspoon salt
1 egg	

Break egg in bowl and beat until light. Add sugar and salt. Alternate the sifted flour and water. Beat again for a few minutes. Heat iron in deep fat. Dip in batter and fry until brown. Use same recipe for Rosettes except, add 1 more egg and 1 more tablespoon of sugar.

PAN CAKES

1 cup sifted flour	½ cup cold water or milk
2 eggs	½ teaspoon salt
2 teaspoons baking powder	2 tablespoons sugar

Beat eggs, add dry ingredients, then cold water or milk. Beat until smooth, drop on hot greased griddle. Turn and brown on both sides. Serve hot with Cane Syrup or jam.

POTATO PANCAKES

2 cups grated potatoes	1 tablespoon flour
3 eggs	½ teaspoon salt

Peel and grate potatoes, put in colander and drain off all water. Do not allow potatoes to stand as this will darken pancakes. Beat potatoes, eggs, flour and salt together. Drop by spoonfuls into ½ inch hot fat. (Test fat by browning a cube of bread 40 seconds). Brown pancake on both sides and serve immediately.

Potato pancakes made in this manner will be light in color, crisp and very tasty.

EGGS AND OMELETS

POACHED EGGS

Butter the bottom of a shallow pan and, in this, add enough boiling, salted water (1 teaspoon salt to 1 quart water) to cover the eggs. Slip eggs, one at a time, into pan, cover and turn flame very low to prevent boiling. Cook 3 to 10 minutes according to degree of firmness desired. Serve on buttered toast, season with salt and dots of butter. A regulation poached-egg ring, well-greased, will hold the eggs in shape and in this case serve on buttered toast cut round. Garnish with small sprigs of parsley.

FRIED EGGS

Heat in frying pan enough butter or fat to cover bottom of pan. Slip eggs into pan, one at a time, and season according to taste. To fry on both sides, turn egg over with spatula or cake turner. Cook slowly to desired firmness.

SCRAMBLED EGGS

4 eggs	1½ teaspoons salt
¼ cup milk	Pepper to taste
1 tablespoon butter	

Stir eggs until mixed. Add seasonings and milk. Heat butter in frying pan, add eggs and cook until creamy. Scrape from bottom of pan as the mixture cooks. Serve on thin buttered toast.

STEWED EGGS AND OYSTERS

6 hard-boiled eggs
2 dozen large oysters
1 tablespoon chopped onion
1 tablespoon chopped parsley
2 tablespoons butter

2 tablespoons cooking oil
1 cup water
1 cup oyster liquor
4 tablespoons flour

Make a roux with flour, oil, butter and onion. Add water to oyster liquor, season with salt and pepper and cook 10 minutes. Then add oysters and eggs split lengthwise with remaining seasonings. Let simmer 10 minutes longer, then serve with rice.

ORANGE OMELET

Ingredients for plain omelet
2 teaspoons lemon juice as substitute for milk

3 tablespoons powdered sugar
Pulp of 2 oranges, skinned

Make omelet according to plain omelet recipe. (Page 38). Substitute lemon juice for milk and add 2 tablespoons to yolk mixture. Place slice of ½ orange slices sprinkled with powdered sugar over half omelet. Fold omelet over, remove from pan and garnish with remainder of orange. Sprinkle again with powdered sugar and serve at once.

SCALLOPED EGGS

3 hard-boiled eggs
2 cups white sauce
½ cup bread crumbs

¾ cup cooked ham, fish, crab-meat or chicken
1 tablespoon butter

Arrange alternate layers of sliced eggs, bread crumbs and ham or other cooked substitute in a buttered baking dish. Pour white sauce over the mixture, cover with bread crumbs, dot with butter and brown in a moderate oven. Serve in baking dish as a main dish for luncheon or supper.

SCALLOPED EGGS AND TOMATOES

6 large firm tomatoes
6 eggs
¼ pound American Cheese

6 slices bacon
Butter
Salt and pepper to taste

Cut off tops of tomatoes and scoop out centers. Place in greased pan. Break whole egg into hollow of each tomato. Sprinkle with salt and pepper and dot with pieces of butter. Bake in oven for fifteen minutes; then remove and sprinkle with grated cheese. Return to oven long enough for cheese to melt. Place on platter and garnish with crisply fried bacon. Serve as a first course or a lunch dish.

STUFFED EGGS

3 hard-boiled eggs
½ teaspoon lemon juice or vinegar
1½ tablespoons melted butter
1 tablespoon mayonnaise

½ teaspoon dry mustard
½ teaspoon salt
½ teaspoon cayenne
Toast crumbs

Cut eggs in half, mash yolks with lemon juice or vinegar, add mustard, salt, cayenne, melted butter and mayonnaise. Refill whites with yolk mixture. Top eggs with finely rolled toast crumbs, or finely chopped parsley.

To vary, sardines, minced ham or chopped crisp bacon may be added to yolk mixture. In such cases more mayonnaise should be added.

CREAMED EGGS

4 hard-boiled eggs sliced
2 tablespoons flour
3 tablespoons butter
1 cup hot milk

½ teaspoon Worcestershire sauce
1 tablespoon chopped parsley
Few drops Tabasco
Salt and pepper to taste

Melt butter, add flour. Add milk slowly. Let cook until thickened about 5 minutes. Then add parsley and seasonings. Place sliced eggs in center of vegetable mould and pour sauce over eggs. Garnish the top with Paprika and serve. Creamed

Eggs may be served on toast as a first course for a luncheon or supper dish. Creamed Mushrooms or Carrots can be made by using same recipe.

PLAIN OMELET

4 eggs	1 tablespoon cooking oil
4 tablespoons milk	½ teaspoon salt
2 tablespoons melted butter	⅛ teaspoon pepper

Beat eggs until light, add milk, salt and pepper. Put oil in frying pan. When hot pour in the eggs and melted butter. When it begins to set, put spatula under and raise slightly allowing some of the uncooked egg to flow under. When omelet begins to get form, let cook two minutes. Then fold over so the two sides meet in center. Turn onto hot dish.

SOUFFLE OMELET

3 tablespoons butter	½ teaspoon cream of tartar
3 eggs	Salt and pepper to taste

Separate eggs, beat yolks until light. Beat white until it begins to foam, add cream of tartar and beat until stiff. Fold yolk into white. Pour into buttered frying pan. When it begins to set put spatula under and fold over so the two sides meet in center. Cook for 2 minutes then put under flame to brown top. Turn onto hot platter.

SPANISH OMELET

1 medium onion	4 tablespoons cooking oil
2 medium sized fresh tomatoes	3 tablespoons butter
or	3 eggs
½ cup canned tomatoes	½ teaspoon cream of tartar
1 sweet pepper	Salt and pepper to taste
1 part garlic	

Chop seasonings (not too fine). Put into sauce pan and cook 10 minutes. Set aside to cool. Just before ready to serve, separate eggs, beat yolks until light, beat white until it begins to foam, add cream of tartar and beat until stiff. Fold yolk into white. Pour into buttered frying pan, add ½ cooked seasonings. When it begins to set, put spatula under and fold over so the two sides meet in center. Cook for 1 minute then put under flame to brown top. Turn onto hot platter and pour remaining of seasonings around and serve immediately. In case of using an omelet pan, pour the eggs on each side of the pan. Pour ½ seasoning on one side. Fold over and cook for 3 minutes on each side. Serve as above.

CRABMEAT OMELET

Use plain omelet recipe (Page 38). Fold crabmeat into the uncooked mixture. Garnish with parsley.

OYSTER OMELET

Use plain omelet recipe (Page 38). Fold oysters into the uncooked mixture. Garnish with parsley.

In either of above, souffle omelet recipe may be used.

SALADS AND
SALAD DRESSINGS

Salads are very rich in minerals and vitamins and should be included daily in the menu.

A salad is always best when served cold, attractive as possible, and with such garnishes as can be eaten.

The green salad is always considered the correct salad for dinner and should be mixed in a large bowl at the table, as no salad made of greens should wait for the eater, and to be refreshing the ingredients should be cool and dry before the seasonings are added.

Have a large bowl, thoroughly washed and dried salad greens, and ready measured seasonings.

There are various kinds of delicious salad dressings which add flavor to the salad itself.

For variety, catsup, Worcestershire sauce, finely chopped onion or chives or paprika may be added, or the bowl rubbed with a clove of garlic.

A large quantity of dressing can be made and bottled and will keep indefinitely if put in a cool place and is always ready for a hasty salad.

GREEN SALADS

Two or more greens, such as:

Lettuce	tomatoes
Water cress	green peppers
chicory	radishes
endive	cucumbers

3 tablespoons salad oil
¾ tablespoon vinegar
½ teaspoon salt
½ teaspoon paprika

⅛ teaspoon Coleman's mustard
Pepper to taste
1 part of garlic

Rub inside of bowl with the cut end of a clove of garlic. Put salad greens into bowl, add oil and, with salad fork and spoon, toss greens until each leaf is coated with oil. Dissolve salt, pepper, paprika and mustard in vinegar in salad spoon. Sprinkle this over greens and toss thoroughly.

VEGETABLE SALAD

1 cup peeled diced tomatoes
1 cup boiled diced carrots
1 cup boiled string beans

1 cup diced cucumbers
1 cup boiled young okra
1 head lettuce

Marinate all the vegetables, except the lettuce, with French Dressings. Serve in a nest of Shredded lettuce.

LILY TOMATOES

4 ripe firm tomatoes
2 packages Philadelphia cream cheese
½ teaspoon salt
½ teaspoon lemon juice

Few drops onion juice
Few drops Tabasco or pinch cayenne
Pinch white pepper

Peel tomatoes with very sharp paring knife. Soften cheese with milk and seasonings, then fill teaspoon with cheese mixture and smooth with back of knife. Press out of spoon on upper side of tomato to form first petal. Continue placing cheese petals around tomato, one up and one down the sides, until it is surrounded by petals. Place in refrigerator until cheese is hardened.

As a variation, cut out center of tomato, fill with shrimp or other salad. Add mayonnaise, serve on lettuce.

[41]

SNOW WHITE SALAD

2 packages Philadelphia cream
  Cheese
¼ pound blanched almonds
  Juice 3 lemons
  Pinch cayenne

½ teaspoon salt
1 can white grapes (pitted)
2 tablespoons gelatine
2 tablespoons sugar
2 cups water

Cream cheese until smooth. Then add sugar, salt, cayenne, lemon juice, grapes and finely chopped almonds. Soak gelatine in a quarter of a cup of cold water. Dissolve this in remaining portion of water, heated, and set aside to cool. Pour dissolved gelatine into other mixed ingredients; stir thoroughly. Pour into a ring mold. Set in refrigerator until firm. Serve on lettuce with mayonnaise.

FROZEN TOMATO SALAD

Boil 2 cups ripe tomatoes for 10 minutes with 2 cloves, 2 tablespoons sugar, 1 tablespoon salt, ¼ teaspoon celery salt, 2 or 3 pepper corns, 1 slice onion, a few grains parsley and 2 tablespoons vinegar. Press through a sieve, freeze to a mush and add ½ cup cream or 1 egg white beaten until stiff. Finish freezing. Serve on a crisp lettuce leaf with mayonnaise or French Dressing or in sherbet glasses as a compote to the meat course.

CHICKEN SALAD

Cut cold boiled chicken into small cubes, place in a bowl and to each quart allow a teaspoon salt, a tablespoon lemon juice or vinegar, ⅛ teaspoon black pepper; mix and chill in refrigerator. To each quart of chicken use 2/3 quart diced celery and let stand in a cold place. Just before serving mix the celery and chicken, cover thoroughly with mayonnaise, serve on lettuce garnished with olives, capers and hard-boiled eggs.

PEAR SALAD

1 package Philadelphia cream cheese
1 large can pears
¼ cup chopped nuts

½ teaspoon salt
2 tablespoons cream
Pink or green vegetable coloring matter if desired.

Mix cheese and cream and add the nuts. Fill centers of two halves of pears with cheese mixture and fasten together with toothpicks at each end. Serve on lettuce with nut dressing.

If more elaborate salad is required, dip one half of pear in coloring matter, leaving other half plain, before filling and fastening halves together. This can be garnished by placing a leaf in one end of pear and a clove in the blossom end. Serve as above.

NUT DRESSING

4 tablespoons finely chopped pecans, almonds or walnuts
4 tablespoons lemon juice
1 teaspoon salt

¼ teaspoon sugar
12 tablespoons salad oil
⅛ teaspoon white pepper
¼ teaspoon paprika

Mix all ingredients and beat well. Add nuts and pour over salad.

CRAB SALAD

½ pound white crabmeat
2 hard-boiled eggs
1 cup finely cut celery
1 tablespoon chopped green pepper

½ teaspoon Worcestershire sauce
Few drops Tabasco
Salt and pepper to taste

Mix all ingredients with the crabmeat and the white of the two hard-boiled eggs, cut fine. Marinate with four tablespoons French Dressing. Add seasonings. Serve in a cup of lettuce. Garnish with mayonnaise dressing and the yolks of the two eggs that have been passed through a sieve. This same salad can be served in tomatoes. Shrimp may be substituted for crab by using the same method.

SHRIMP SALAD

Refer to Crab Salad. Use the same ingredients, substituting shrimps for crabmeat.

CAULIFLOWER AND SHRIMP SALAD

1 large cauliflower	1 head lettuce
2 pounds large *or*	1 cup mayonnaise
3 pounds small boiled shrimp	

Cut cauliflower stem off and cook in boiling water, as usual. Drain, and when cold, place stem-end down on a bed of lettuce. Remove black vein from each shrimp, carefully. Cover cauliflower with mayonnaise and garnish with clusters of shrimp.

LOBSTER SALAD

1 cup flaked lobster	3 tablespoons French Dressing
2 cups diced celery	½ cup mayonnaise
3 hard-boiled eggs	

Marinate lobster with French Dressing, let stand 30 minutes. Drain. Mix with celery, and mayonnaise, arrange on lettuce leaves and garnish with curled celery and sliced hard-boiled eggs.

FROZEN CHEESE AND ANCHOVY SALAD

2 packages Philadelphia cream cheese	½ teaspoon salt
	½ cup mayonnaise
1 small bottle whole anchovies	¼ cup cream
½ cup chopped pimentoes	Few drops Tabasco
½ teaspoon Worcestershire sauce	

Cream the cheese. Drain oil from anchovies and chop fine. Then add anchovies and finely choped pimentoes to cheese. Add remaining ingredients and stir. Pour in any ordinary round can with tight cover, approximately 4 inches in diameter. Pack and freeze in ice and salt for one hour.

To serve: Remove can from ice and wash salt under cold

water. Coax frozen mixture out of can with knife if necessary. Cut slices ½ inch thick and serve with mayonnaise or cooked cream dressing on bed of lettuce.

JELLIED CABBAGE AND PIMENTO SALAD

2 cups shredded white cabbage
½ cup finely chopped pimento
½ cup finely chopped celery
¼ cup vinegar
¼ cup brown sugar
2 level tablespoons gelatine
1 cup cold water

Soak gelatine in ½ cup cold water. Heat the vinegar and stir in to dissolve the gelatine. Add the brown sugar, cold water, cabbage, pimento and celery. Stir well. Pour into a square pan, and chill in ice box until firm. Cut into large squares and serve with mayonnaise on lettuce. This salad can also be molded in individual molds.

JELLIED CUCUMBER AND PINEAPPLE SALAD

2 cups crushed pineapple
1 cup finely diced cucumber
¼ cup lemon juice
¼ cup sugar
2 tablespoons gelatine
1½ cups water
1 teaspoon salt

Soak gelatine in one-half cup cold water. Heat the remainder of the water and in this dissolve the gelatine. Add the sugar, salt, cucumber, pineapple and lemon juice. Stir well. Put into whole or individual molds and chill in ice box until firm. Serve on a bed of lettuce with mayonnaise or cream dressing.

GRAPEFRUIT AND ORANGE SALAD

3 large grapefruits
3 large oranges
Small can pimento
Lettuce
Parsley

Peel oranges and grapefruits and remove membranes from sections. Arrange slices side by side on lettuce leaves, with narrow edges down, alternating orange and grapefruit. Mark divisions of slices with strips of pimento. Garnish with curly parsley and serve with French Dressing (Page 53). This will serve six.

STUFFED HEARTS OF ARTICHOKES SALAD

Following directions for boiling artichokes. When cold, pull out leaves and remove choke with a silver teaspoon. Scrape the artichokes from the tip end of the leaves. Mix with a little mayonnaise, lemon juice, chopped celery, salt and pepper to taste. Serve on a leaf or shredded lettuce or with Fluffy Egg Dressing (Page 53).

POTATO SALAD

2 pounds potatoes
1 tablespoon chopped onion
2 tablespoons chopped parsley
¼ cup French Dressing

1 cup chopped celery
1 cup mayonnaise
Salt and pepper to taste

Boil the potatoes in their jackets and allow them to cool before peeling. Cut into small pieces and mix with parsley, onion, French dressing, celery, mayonnaise, salt and pepper to taste.

Old-fashioned potato salad can be made in the same way using one-half cup of French dressing and four chopped hard-boiled eggs. Omit the mayonnaise.

CHICKEN ASPIC

2 cups diced chicken
½ cup pimento
½ cup finely chopped olives
2 tablespoons gelatine

3 cups meat or chicken stock
½ cup cold water
1 teaspoon Worcestershire sauce
Salt and pepper to taste

Heat the stock and in this dissolve the gelatine which has been soaked in cold water for 5 minutes. Mix the chicken, pimento, olives, Worcestershire sauce, salt and pepper Stir into stock and pour mixture into individual molds. Chill in ice box until firm and serve on lettuce leaf with mayonnaise.

CLEAR ASPIC

1 tablespoon gelatine   1 pint chicken or beef stock
¼ cup cold water

Soak gelatine in cold water for 5 minutes. Season stock with salt and pepper, heat and stir in gelatine until dissolved. Pour into one large mold or individual ones which have been moistened with cold water. When cool, place in ice box to become firm. Serve with mayonnaise on crisp lettuce and garnish with strips of pimento. If ring mold is used, fill center with cole slaw or other salad.

CRAB ASPIC

2 cups crabmeat   2 tablespoons lemon juice
1 cup finely chopped celery   1 teaspoon Worcestershire sauce
2 tablespoons gelatine   Few drops Tabasco
2 cups tomato juice   Salt and pepper to taste
½ cup cold water

Heat tomato and lemon juices. Then add gelatine which has been soaked in cold water for 5 minutes. Mix crabmeat, celery, Worcestershire sauce, Tabasco, salt and pepper. Stir into first mixture and pour into individual or whole molds. Chill in ice box until firm and serve on lettuce leaf with mayonnaise.

CLEAR FRUIT ASPIC

¼ cup cold water   1 cup grapefruit juice
¼ cup boiling water   1 tablespoon lemon juice
1 tablespoon gelatine   ¼ cup sugar.

Put grapefruit juice and lemon juice and rind in sauce pan with hot water. Let come to boiling point. Add sugar and gelatine which has been soaked in cold water for 5 minutes. Remove from fire. Color with vegetable coloring if desired. Pour into individual or whole mold. Place in refrigerator to congeal.

Fill center with shrimp, crab or fresh fruit. Serve on lettuce with mayonnaise or cream dressing.

TOMATO ASPIC

2 cups canned tomatoes	2 sprigs celery
1 chopped onion	2 sprigs parsley
1 bay leaf	1 pod garlic
½ lemon (juice)	4½ cups water
2 cloves	4 tablespoons gelatine
1 whole all spice	Salt and pepper to taste
1 sprig thyme	

Soak gelatine in ½ cup cold water for 5 minutes. Boil remainder of ingredients for 15 minutes. Strain through a cloth. Stir in gelatine and dissolve. This may be placed in whole or individual molds. Chill in refrigerator until firm.

AVOCADO OR ALLIGATOR PEAR ASPIC

2 cups diced avocado or alligator pear	¼ cup cold water
2 tablespoons gelatine	1 pint well seasoned chicken or beef stock

Soak gelatine in cold water for 5 minutes. Heat beef stock and dissolve gelatine in it. When liquid cools add avocado. Place in mold and jell in refrigerator. Serve on bed of lettuce with mayonnaise or cooked dressing.

PINEAPPLE AND CHEESE SALAD

Mix 1 cake of Pimento cheese with a little pineapple juice until creamy. Beat lightly until fluffy and put in center of pineapple rings on crisp lettuce leaves. Serve with French dressing.

COLE SLAW

To 2 cups of finely shredded white cabbage add 1 teaspoon sugar, 2 tablespoons mayonnaise. Marinate with French dressing.

ARTICHOKE MOUSSE

6 Artichokes	2½ cups water
1 cup mayonnaise	½ lemon
1 cup whipped cream	¼ teaspoon cayenne pepper
2 tablespoons gelatine	Salt to taste

Boil artichokes in a large pot of water with a ½ lemon until tender. Remove from fire and drain. When cool separate leaves from heart and scrape leaves. Cut heart in small pieces. Soak gelatine in half cup cold water, let stand five minutes. Dissolve gelatine in remaining 2 cups hot water. When gelatine has dissolved mix all ingredients, pour into a mold. Place in ice box to congeal. When firm, serve on a bed of lettuce with mayonnaise dressing.

GROUND ARTICHOKE MOUSSE

2 cups ground artichokes	1 tablespoon vinegar
½ cup chopped olives	3 tablespoons gelatine
½ cup chopped nuts	1 cup hot meat stock
½ cup chopped pimento	½ cup cold water
1 cup mayonnaise	Salt, white pepper and cayen-
1 cup whipped cream	ne to taste

Boil and mash ground artichokes. Soak gelatine in cold water. Dissolve in the cup of hot meat stock. Stir all ingredients together and pour over all the gelatine mixture. Put into a mold and chill in ice box until firm. Serve on a bed of lettuce with mayonnaise or cream dressing. This constitutes a delicious first course for any dinner or luncheon.

CHICKEN MOUSSE

1 cup cooked white chicken meat ground very fine	¼ teaspoon salt
	½ pint cream, whipped
1 cup chicken broth	½ cup mayonnaise
3 egg yolks	Few grains paprika
1 tablespoon gelatine	Pepper to taste

Soak gelatine for 5 minutes in ½ cup cold broth. Beat yolks of eggs and stir lightly into remainder of broth, add seasonings and cook in double boiler until thickened to custard consistency. Dissolve softened gelatine in broth and egg mixture. Pour this over chicken and stir over ice-water until mousse begins to set, then fold in whipped cream and mayonnaise. Turn into mold which has been moistened with cold water, let stiffen and serve cold garnished with parsley, water-cress or lettuce. This recipe serves six.

JELLIED SHRIMP SALAD

1 quart canned tomatoes	1 teaspoon mustard
1¼ cups water	2 tablespoons granulated gela-
1½ teaspoons salt	tine
¼ teaspoon pepper	1½ cups boiled shrimp
4 cloves	½ cup finely diced celery
1 bay leaf	¼ cup diced green pepper
1 tablespoon sugar	1 small onion minced

Cook the tomatoes and spices, one cup water and onion for fifteen minutes. Strain, and pour over the gelatine which has been softened in ¼ cup cold water. Cool and when it begins to stiffen add the shrimps which have been cleaned and black veins removed and cut in pieces. Then add the celery and the pepper. Pour into individual molds, chill in ice box. Serve on beds of lettuce with mayonnaise or cooked dressing.

FROZEN FRUIT SALAD

2 cakes Philadelphia Cream Cheese	1 cup diced pineapple
	½ cup chopped nuts
1 teaspoon Worcestershire sauce	1 small bottle maraschino cher-
1 cup mayonnaise	ries (drain and chop)
1 cup whipped cream	1 head lettuce
¼ cup sugar	

Soften cream cheese with Worcestershire sauce, mayonnaise and whipped cream. Mix well with nuts, sugar and fruits. Pack in mold and freeze, or put in refrigerator freezing unit for several hours. Serve on lettuce leaf with toasted crackers.

RAW VEGETABLE SALAD

1 cup of grated raw carrots
1 cup shredded raw cabbage
½ cup finely chopped celery

2 teaspoons lemon juice
1 teaspoon salt
3 tablespoons mayonnaise

Combine all ingredients together and serve on lettuce leaf.

SPINACH SALAD

3 cups boiled cooked spinach passed through seive and drained.

Dressing for Salad:

4½ tablespoons salad oil
1½ tablespoons lemon juice
½ tablespoon chopped onions
⅓ teaspoon mustard

1 teaspoon salt
⅛ teaspoon pepper
A few drops Worcestershire
sauce

Combine spinach and dressing together, chill in ice box, serve on lettuce leaf.

MAYONNAISE DRESSING

1 egg yolk
½ teaspoon salt
1 cup olive oil
(or any other brand of salad
oil serves as well)

1 tablespoon lemon juice
1 tablespoon vinegar
½ teaspoon dry mustard (if desired)
Few grains cayenne pepper

Have mixture bowl and all ingredients very cold. Stir the yolk with a fork, add a portion of the lemon juice, stir and add oil drop by drop, stirring constantly, add other ingredients, and as mixture thickens add alternately, lemon juice and oil.

ROQUEFORT CHEESE DRESSING
(Six portions)

1/3 cup Roquefort cheese
1/3 cup salad oil
½ teaspoon dry mustard
1 tablespoon vinegar

½ teaspoon salt
½ teaspoon paprika
¼ teaspoon sugar

[51]

Cream the cheese. Slowly add the oil until a soft creamy mixture is formed. Mix the mustard, paprika, sugar and salt, and add to the cheese mixture. Then add the vinegar and beat well. Serve on sliced tomatoes, a quarter of a head of lettuce, cooked asparagus or halves of canned peaches arranged on lettuce.

THOUSAND ISLAND DRESSING

¾ cup mayonnaise dressing
2 tablespoons finely chopped red and green pepper
2 tablespoons chili sauce
1 hard boiled egg finely chopped

1 teaspoon Worcestershire sauce
1 tablespoon catsup
½ teaspoon paprika
¼ cup whipped cream

Mix all the ingredients and when ready to serve add mayonnaise and whipped cream.

COOKED MAYONNAISE DRESSING

1 cup oil
2 egg yolks } Put in bowl
2 tablespoons flour
2 tablespoons vinegar
1 tablespoon sugar

1 teaspoon salt
1 teaspoon paprika
1 teaspoon dry mustard
juice of 1 lemon
1 cup hot water

Make a paste of the flour and the dry ingredients and vinegar and lemon. Gradually add the hot water and cook over boiling water or in a double boiler for five minutes or until it clears up.

Put eggs and oil in a bowl and add the cooked paste and beat with a Dover egg beater until creamy.

This dressing may be varied by adding whipped cream, for fruit salad, or as a foundation for thousand island dressing add chili sauce, chopped onion, chives, pepper or minced hard boiled egg.

FRENCH DRESSING

4 tablespoons salad oil
1½ to 2 tablespoons lemon juice
   or mild vinegar

1 teaspoon salt
⅛ teaspoon paprika

Mix vinegar and dry ingredients, add a small piece of ice, and beat with a silver fork or shake in a covered jar until it is thick and creamy. Serve immediately.

Spanish Dressing: Add 2 tablespoons catsup to French Dressing.

FLUFFY EGG DRESSING

4 hard-boiled eggs
5 tablespoons mayonnaise
½ teaspoon lemon juice

½ teaspoon Worcestershire sauce
Salt and pepper to taste

Boil eggs and press through a sieve. Add mayonnaise and seasonings. Beat until fluffy.

CREAM CHEESE DRESSING

¼ cup salad oil
2 tablespoons vinegar
½ teaspoon dry mustard
1 teaspoon finely chopped onion

½ teaspoon sugar
1 teaspoon salt
1 tablespoon chopped parsley
¼ cup cream cheese

Mix the oil and vinegar in a jar. Blend the mustard, sugar and salt, and combine with the first mixture. Add the onion, parsley and cheese which has been creamed until soft. Place lid on jar and shake for 3 minutes. This dressing may be served on the following salads: lettuce, sliced tomatoes, canned pears or peaches.

CREAM DRESSING

Mix equal parts of mayonnaise and whipping cream together. Serve on salad.

[53]

STUFFED CELERY

1 large stalk celery
3 Philadelphia cream cheese
½ cup finely chopped nuts
4 tablespoons sweet cream

¼ teaspoon Worcestershire sauce
½ teaspoon lemon juice
½ teaspoon onion juice
Salt and pepper to taste

Separate and wash the stems of the celery. Cut large stems in half across. Mash Philadelphia cheese with sweet cream and other seasonings. Stir until creamy. Stuff the stems with this mixture placing a small leaf at one end of each stem.

MEATS AND SAUCES

BAKED HAM WITH PASTRY

Ham (14-15) pounds	½ teaspoon nutmeg
2 teaspoons cinnamon	1 onion
1 tablespoon Coleman's mustard	1 part garlic
½ cup vinegar	2 bay leaves
1 piece celery	1 sprig thyme
1 teaspoon cloves	1 quart water
1 teaspoon all-spice	

Soak ham in cold water over night with skin on. Place in baking pan, still without removing skin, in moderate 350° oven. Pour in water and add vinegar, celery, onion, bay leaves, thyme and garlic. Bake in oven, allowing twenty minutes for each pound of ham. Baste four or five times while baking. One hour before ham is to be finished, remove from oven, remove skin and let cool. Rub thoroughly with powdered spices and mustard. Wrap pastry around ham, prick with fork to prevent rising, joining pastry at bottom or side. Cover pastry with well-greased and floured paper. Put back in oven and let bake for last hour, removing paper just before hour is up so as to brown pastry.

PASTRY FOR HAM

6 cups flour	½ cup shortening
1 teaspoon salt	1½ cups cold water
2 tablespoons baking powder	

Sift dry ingredients into a bowl. Cut shortening in with two silver knives until well mixed. Add water slowly, mixing with a fork. Let dough stand for a few minutes, preferably in refrigerator before rolling. Coat rolling pin and board lightly with flour. Pat dough into ball on board and roll lightly from center to edges until one-quarter inch thick. Then proceed as in recipe for Baked Ham with Pastry.

STUFFED PORK CHOPS

Have lean loin chops 1 inch thick. Cut a pocket in center of each chop to the bone for stuffing. Season chops with salt and pepper. Fill center with dressing, holding together with toothpicks.

Roll stuffed chops in flour, dot with butter. Place in baking dish, let brown for 15 minutes in 450° oven, then add water and reduce heat to 325° and cook 45 minutes longer. Baste four times while cooking. If water dries add a little more for gravy.

BREAD STUFFING

Plain

1 cup minced stale bread	1 egg
1 tablespoon chopped onion	2 tablespoons butter
1 tablespoon chopped green pepper	2 tablespoons shortening
¼ teaspoon chopped garlic	½ cup water
2 tablespoons chopped parsley	¼ teaspoon cayenne
1 tablespoon chopped celery	Salt and pepper to taste

Mix all ingredients together, stir thoroughly. Fry in two tablespoons butter and two tablespoons shortening a few minutes.

Following additions may be made for a finer stuffing:

1 cup chopped oysters	2 tablespoons sausages, skinned
Giblets boiled and cut	1 cup chestnuts, chopped

This stuffing may be used for chicken, varieties of meats, or fish.

ROAST BEEF OR VEAL

3 lb. roast (rib, rump or chuck)　　2 parts garlic
2 tbps. of flour　　　　　　　　　　1½ cups of hot water
3 tbps. of cooking oil or vege-
　table fat

Wipe meat with damp cloth, season with salt and pepper. Cut garlic in quarters and stick through meat. Melt fat in roaster or iron pot; place meat in melted fat, sprinkle with flour, let brown on all sides. Add water and cook slowly for one and one-half hours.

For rare meat cook from 45 to 50 minutes.

Pork roast may be cooked in same method but must be well done.

CREOLE FRIED CHICKEN

1 Spring Chicken (2 to 2½　　1 tsp. white pepper
　pounds)　　　　　　　　　　2 tsp. salt
2 eggs　　　　　　　　　　　½ cup flour
¼ cup milk　　　　　　　　　1½ cups cracker meal

Wash, split and cut the chicken in quarters. Season with salt and pepper. Make an egg wash with eggs, milk and one-half teaspoon of salt. Pour the egg wash over the chicken and let it stand about an hour or two. Roll chicken in flour and cracker meal which has been mixed together. Fry in medium hot fat from 12 to 15 minutes.

COUNTRY FRIED CHICKEN

Use the same ingredients used in Creole Fried Chicken with the exception of the cracker meal.

In preparing the chicken follow the same method as in Creole fried chicken.

DAUBE GLACE

2 pounds lean young beef
1 small piece of celery
2 large onions
2 bay leaves
2 sprigs thyme
2 pods garlic

2 lemons
Shells of 2 eggs
4 tablespoons gelatine
Salt, black pepper and
cayenne pepper to taste.

Soak gelatine in one cup of cold water for five minutes. Boil meat and seasonings in 4 quarts of water until liquid is reduced to 1 quart. Remove meat and cut into small pieces. Strain the remainder of the water, add the two lemons cut in half and squeeze. To clarify, add crushed eggshells and boil for a few minutes longer. Strain again through a thick cloth, darken with a few drops of caramel coloring or Kitchen Bouquet and add gelatine. Pour over meat and let chill until firm.

One veal knuckle or 2 calves feet may be used with only 3 tablespoons gelatine for same result.

DAUBE WITH GRAVY

3 pounds beef or veal shoulder,
   rump or round
4 tablespoons flour
½ cup shortening
1 large onion (chopped)
½ teaspoon garlic (chopped)
1 green pepper (chopped)
1 bay leaf

1 sprig parsley
4 cups water
1 sprig thyme
1 cup tomatoes
3 tablespoons celery
2 cups diced carrots
1 cup diced turnips
Salt and pepper to taste

Carrots or turnips or both may be added. Brown meat on all sides in shortening. Remove meat from pot and make a roux by adding flour and onion to remaining shortening. Add water and other seasonings and put meat back in pot. If carrots and turnips are used dice and add 30 minutes before meat is done.

VEAL LOAF

1 pound ground veal	½ teaspoon finely chopped
½ pound ground pickle meat	garlic
½ pound fresh pork (ground)	2 tablespoons finely chopped
2 eggs	parsley
1 cup bread crumbs	4 tablespoons flour
2 tablespoons finely chopped	4 tablespoons shortening
onion	

Mix seasonings with meat in a bowl. Form into two loaves. Sprinkle with flour and dot with shortening. Place in well-greased pan and bake in 350° oven for 25 minutes. When browned, add 1 cup water for gravy a few minutes before removing from pan. Baste four times while baking. These loaves are delicious served hot or cold.

BAKED BROILERS

4 1¼-pound chickens	¼ teaspoon finely chopped gar-
8 tablespoons cooking oil	lic
2 cups cream	½ cup mushroom water
1 cup mushrooms	Salt and pepper

Dress and split the chickens down the back. Wash and season with salt and pepper to taste. Roll in flour. Place in baking pan skin side up in hot oven (450° F.). Pour one tablespoon cooking oil on each half chicken. Cook twenty minutes, basting four times during the period. Remove from oven. Mix together the cream, mushrooms, mushroom water and garlic. Return to oven and let cook ten more minutes, basting at least twice during that time. Serve on platter on pieces of dry toast if desired. Garnish with parsley or water cress.

For broiled or fried chicken halves: Always cut joint of drumstick slightly and bend, so that the half chicken can fit better on a piece of toast.

TURKEY WITH SPAGHETTI

8 slices breast of turkey or chicken	½ cup canned mushrooms
¼ pound spaghetti	Salt
½ pint whipping cream	Cayenne pepper
½ pint turkey stock	White pepper
⅛ pound butter	¼ cup sherry
2 tablespoons flour	Yolk of 1 egg

Break spaghetti in half. Put 1½ teaspoons salt in 5 cups boiling water. Cook spaghetti in this for 15 minutes. Drain off water and let cold water run over cooked spaghetti to remove excess starch.

Prepare cream sauce by blending flour in melted butter, add turkey stock, then the cream, mushrooms, 1⅛ teaspoons salt, ¼ teaspoon cayenne and a pinch of white pepper. Cook about 10 minutes until thickened.

Line baking or pyrex dish with slices of turkey, then a layer of spaghetti, another layer of turkey and spaghetti over this. Add well-beaten yolk of egg and sherry to the sauce and pour over turkey and spaghetti. Dot with butter. Bake in upper part of 350° oven for 15 to 20 minutes, or until slightly browned.

CREAMED CHICKEN A LA KING

½ cup butter	1 cup chicken broth
½ cup flour	2 egg yolks
1 cup milk	2 tablespoons lemon juice
1 cup mushrooms	¼ teaspoon mustard
¼ cup green pepper	2 teaspoons salt
2 cups diced cooked chicken	1 teaspoon paprika
¼ cup pimento	

Make white sauce by blending butter and flour, and adding hot milk. Cook and stir until thickened. Saute mushrooms and add to sauce with minced green pepper and chicken. Beat egg yolks, add seasonings, and add to rest of mixture. Heat until the boiling point is reached and simmer slowly ten minutes.

POT ROAST WILD DUCK

Clean and dress the duck. Cut into pieces for serving and soak in cold salted water for a few hours, to which one tablespoon of soda has been added. Remove from water, sprinkle with salt and pepper, and dredge in flour. Fry in hot fat until a golden brown. Remove and place in a roaster adding two cups of hot water for gravy. Cover tightly and roast in a 250° oven, until tender, for one hour.

MARYLAND CHICKEN

Prepare chicken as for frying. Put the neck and giblets into cold water and let simmer on slow fire to obtain cup of stock for gravy. Dip pieces of chicken in well-beaten egg and bread crumbs. Place in greased pan and dot with butter or shortening. Let cook in oven at 450° for 15 minutes until partly browned, then add cup of stock and baste frequently. Cook for another 15 minutes. Mushrooms may be added to make a richer gravy.

GRILLADES PANEES

1 veal round	1½ teaspoon salt
2 beaten eggs	½ teaspoon pepper
2 cups cracker or bread crumbs	¼ cup milk

Cut veal round into individual pieces. Remove extra fat and dip meat into crumbs and then in mixture of eggs, milk and seasonings, and roll in crumbs again. Fry in deep fat until brown.

ROAST LAMB OR MUTTON

1 leg of mutton or lamb	Salt and pepper
Flour	

Wipe the meat with a damp cloth. Remove the outer skin and excess fat. Sprinkle with salt, pepper and flour, and place in a roasting pan, in a very hot 450° oven. After 15 minutes, reduce the heat for the rest of the cooking period. Allow 20 minutes, to a pound for roasting. When done, remove meat from oven. Also remove all fat except one tablespoon and, in this, brown 2 tablespoons flour, add one and one-half cups of boiling water and stir until it thickens. Cook gravy for two minutes, season to taste and strain. If the roast is from the breast, it may be stuffed with Bread Stuffing or Nut Stuffing. (See page 56).

LENA'S LAMB CHOPS AND PINEAPPLE

8 lamb chops	¼ teaspoon white pepper
½ teaspoon salt	8 slices pineapple

Pan broil the chops well browned. Sprinkle with salt. Place the pineapple slices under browned chops and broil for 10 minutes. Serve on a platter garnished with parsley. Baste the chops several times during the broiling.

HAM AND POTATO CROQUETTES

1 cup minced cooked ham	2 eggs
2 cups mashed potatoes	½ cup dry bread crumbs
1 tablespoon chopped onion	¼ teaspoon cayenne pepper
1 tablespoon chopped green pepper	Salt to taste

Separate eggs, beating the yolks, and then slightly beat the whites in ¼ cup water. Combine ham and yolks and barely heat while stirring constantly. Cool, shape into eight small balls, and entirely cover each ball with mashed potato. Roll in fine dry crumbs, dip in white of egg, roll in bread crumbs again, fry in deep fat and drain. This recipe serves six people.

BAKED HAM
With Brown Sugar

1 ham (16 to 18 pounds)	2 pods garlic
2 sprigs celery	½ cup vinegar
2 bay leaves	5 cups water
1 sprig thyme	2 cups brown sugar
6 whole cloves	Sliced canned pineapple
6 whole all spice	Sliced oranges
1 medium sized onion	

Place ham in covered baking pan, pour in water and vinegar. Add to this the celery, bay leaves, thyme, cloves, all spice, garlic and onion. Cook four hours basting four times in 350° oven. Remove ham from oven and, when cool, remove the skin. Let ham partly brown under slow flame. Remove ham, and sprinkle brown sugar over it. Garnish with cloves, sliced canned pineapple, or sliced oranges. Again place ham in oven under slow flame until sugar is browned and dried. This is a very attractive way to serve a ham and will serve 30 people.

CREAMED SWEETBREADS

1 pair sweetbreads
1 can mushrooms
4 tablespoons butter
  Tabasco
  Chopped parsley
  Shallots

1 cup milk
¼ cup mushroom liquor
3 tablespoons flour
  Worcestershire sauce
  Sherry (2 tablespoons)
  Yolks 2 eggs

Soak sweetbreads in cold water for 30 minutes. Drain. Cover with hot salted water to which one tablespoon lemon juice or vinegar has been added. Simmer about 30 minutes. Drain and plunge into cold water. Remove membranes and divide into pieces.

Prepare cream sauce by blending flour in butter. Add hot milk slowly, then mushroom liquor. Add mushrooms and sweetbreads. Let simmer for 10 minutes. Add well-beaten eggs and sherry just before removing from fire.

Creamed sweetbreads may be used as stuffing for artichokes.

SCALLOPED SWEETBREADS AND MUSHROOMS

1 pound sweetbreads
1 can mushrooms
1 cup cracker crumbs
1 teaspoon finely chopped onion
1 tablespoon meat stock
¼ teaspoon minced garlic
1 teaspoon chopped green peper

1 teaspoon salt
¼ teaspoon cayenne pepper
2 tablespoons butter
2 tablespoons flour
2 cups milk
1 cup mushroom liquor
1 pimento shredded

[63]

Soak sweetbreads in cold water for 30 minutes. Drain. Cover with hot salted water to which one tablespoon lemon juice or vinegar has been added. Simmer 15 minutes. Drain and plunge into cold water. Remove membranes and divide into pieces.

Make a thin white sauce by adding flour and seasonings to the melted butter, gradually adding the milk then mushroom liquor and stock, stirring constantly. Place layers of sweetbreads, mushrooms and ½ cracker crumbs in a buttered baking dish. Pour sauce over this, cover with remaining crumbs and dot with butter. Bake in a 350° oven for 25 minutes.

BRUNSWICK STEW IN VOL-AU-VENT OR RING OF RICE

2½ to 3 pounds spring chicken
1 cup fresh or canned corn
3 fresh tomatoes (cut in quarters)
6 small onions
12 small new potatoes (left whole)
½ cup diced carrots
24 string beans
½ cup diced turnips
1½ cups water
½ cup shortening
½ teaspoon garlic
1 bay leaf
1 sprig thyme
2 green peppers, (cut in large pieces)
¼ cup flour
Salt and pepper to taste

Wash and disjoint chicken, fry in shortening until light brown. Remove chicken from saucepan. Make a roux, using the same shortening. Add all ingredients except corn and let cook for twenty minutes in a covered iron pot or casserole. Then add corn, simmer five to ten minutes longer. Serve in Vol-au-vent (Page 136). Rice ring may be substituted for Vol-au-vent.

PLAIN BROILED CHICKEN

Use chickens weighing 1¼ to 1½ pounds each and have them dressed and split for broiling. Wash and place in a well-greased pan, skin side down, with pieces of butter on top. Sprinkle with salt and white or black pepper. Put in hot upper oven (450° Fahrenheit) and bake one half hour, turning at least twice while cooking. Remove to a well-greased wire broiler and cook over a clear fire or under the fire in a broiling oven to brown. When done, serve on pieces of dry toast, brush with melted butter and lemon juice, sprinkle with chopped parsley and garnish with water cress and slices of lemon.

BREAST OF TURKEY OR CHICKEN WITH SWEETBREAD AND HAM SAUCE

8 squares of toast
8 slices of cooked breast of turkey
½ pound raw ham
1 pound sweetbreads
1 cup canned mushrooms
3 tablespoons flour
¼ pound butter

½ teaspoon garlic
2 tablespoons chopped green pepper
2 tablespoons chopped onion
2 cups water
Juice of 1 lemon
Salt and pepper to taste

Prepare sweetbreads as in sweetbread recipe. Make a roux with the butter, flour and onion. Add chopped raw ham, mushrooms, sweetbreads, garlic and sweet pepper. Add salt and pepper, then let simmer in water for twenty minutes.

Line a platter with squares of toast and sliced turkey. Add lemon juice to sauce and pour over turkey. Sprinkle with chopped parsley and serve.

ROAST TURKEY

1 medium-sized turkey (10 or 12 pounds)
2 tablespoons cooking oil
2 tablespoons butter

4 tablespoons flour
Salt and pepper to taste
Oyster Stuffing

Wash turkey, remove all pin feathers, singe and clean thoroughly. Fill with stuffing. Cross the drumsticks, tie them securely with a long string and fasten to the tail. Dredge the bird with flour, salt and pepper, pour over oil and butter and place in a roaster in hot (450°) oven to finish baking. Bake sixty minutes longer. Baste the turkey frequently while baking. This same method can be used for roasting chicken, goose or duck.

The oyster stuffing is considered by Lena to be the most delicious turkey stuffing because the flavor of the oyster permeates the turkey. Any other stuffing may be used with excellent results.

BREADED VEAL CHOPS OR GRILLADES PANEES

6 veal chops *or*
2 veal rounds
2 beaten eggs
2 cups cracker meal

1½ teaspoons salt
½ teaspoon pepper
¼ cup milk

Select loin chops or round steaks. Cut round steaks into individual pieces. Season. Remove extra fat and dip meat into egg wash (Page 135) and then in cracker meal, back into egg wash and then cracker meal again. Fry in deep fat until brown.

BROILED PORTERHOUSE OR TENDERLOIN STEAK

Trim steak, then lay on greased broiler under very hot flame. Sear on one side, season, turn once without piercing the meat, sear on other side, then lower rack and cook "well done" or rare as desired. Serve on hot platter with melted butter and chopped parsley, or Fresh Mushroom Sauce (Page 70). Garnish with slices of lemon.

GRILLADE A LA CREOLE

1 pound veal round
1 cup canned tomatoes *or*
3 fresh tomatoes (chopped)
1 medium sized onion (chopped)
1 medium green pepper (chopped)
1 pod chopped garlic

1 sprig thyme
1 bay leaf
1 tablespoon parsley
½ cup shortening
4 tablespoons flour
1½ cups water
Salt and pepper to taste

Cut veal round in pieces and fry in shortening until brown. Remove from shortening and make a roux with the remaining fat, flour and onion. Add tomatoes and simmer a few minutes. Add meat, water and other ingredients and cook 15 or 20 minutes. This serves four people. It has always been a custom to serve Grillade with rice.

FILET MIGNON

Use very choice tenderloin and wrap each steak with a strip of bacon. Broil as in steak recipe.

MEAT AND VEGETABLE STEW

1 pound beef or veal	3 slices onion
¾ cup diced potatoes	½ cup diced turnips
¾ cup diced carrots	1 teaspoon salt
3 tablespoons flour	¼ teaspoon cayenne pepper
3 tablespoons bacon fat	

Cut meat into 1 inch cubes, roll in flour and brown in bacon fat in frying pan. Cover meat with water and boil for one hour, until meat is almost cooked. Add vegetables and seasonings and let simmer for twenty minutes.

STUFFED BROILERS

3 broilers (1½ pounds each)	¾ cup oyster water or ordinary water
6 slices fried chopped bacon	3 tablespoons shortening
2 tablespoons chopped onion	2 tablespoons butter
½ teaspoon chopped garlic	1 tablespoon chopped celery
2 tablespoons chopped green pepper	2 tablespoons chopped parsley
1 dozen chopped oysters	¼ teaspoon cayenne pepper
1 cup bread crumbs	Salt and pepper to taste

Mix all ingredients together, except water and bread crumbs. Fry in shortening and butter. Add water and bread crumbs, stir well then add seasonings.

Dress and split the chickens down the back. Wash and season with 1 tablespoon salt and ½ teaspoon pepper. Place in

[67]

greased baking pan, skin side down. Add ½ cup water to prevent sticking. Place one large spoonful of stuffing in each half chicken, smooth well. Sprinkle with bread crumbs and dot with butter. Bake in a 350° oven from 35 to 40 minutes. Garnish with chopped parsley and serve piping hot.

CHICKEN CROQUETTE

2 cups cooked chicken
1 cup milk
4 tablespoons flour
3 tablespoons butter
1 teaspoon finely chopped celery

1 teaspoon lemon juice
1 teaspoon finely chopped onion
1 teaspoon chopped parsley
1 egg
1½ cups cracker meal

Make a white sauce with butter, flour and milk. Add fowl and all the seasonings. Remove from fire and pour in a flat pan and let cool. Then place in the ice box for at least an hour or more. Shape into croquettes and dip into Egg Wash (page 135) and then in cracker meal and again in Egg Wash and again into cracker meal. Fry in deep fat from 3 to 5 minutes.

FRIED BACON

Put 1 teaspoon of cooking oil or shortening in skillet or frying pan. Lay strips of bacon in the pan and fry over a medium flame until crisp. Remove from grease immediately and place on a piece of absorbent paper and serve.

RECIPE FOR MEDIUM CREAM SAUCE

2 tablespoons flour
2 tablespoons butter
1 cup milk

¼ teaspoon salt
⅛ teaspoon pepper

Melt the butter, add the flour and cook until it bubbles. Then add hot milk. Stir constantly while cooking until the sauce thickens.

SAUCE REMOULADE

4 hard-boiled eggs
1 teaspoon dry Coleman's mustard
2 tablespoons chopped parsley
2 tablespoons chopped green pepper
¼ teaspoon finely chopped garlic

1 tablespoon anchovy paste
1 teaspoon Worcestershire sauce
1 cup mayonnaise
6 finely chopped stuffed olives
Salt and pepper to taste

Mince eggs. Add the other ingredients and stir well. This Rémoulade can be served as a salad dressing with shrimp or crab meat on lettuce leaves.

LEMON AND BUTTER SAUCE

4 tablespoons butter
1 tablespoon lemon juice
2 teaspoons chopped parsley

¼ teaspoon salt
⅛ teaspoon paprika

Melt butter, stir in lemon juice, parsley and seasonings.

TARTAR SAUCE

2 tablespoons pickle relish
2 tablespoons chopped ripe olives
1 tablespoon chopped chives
1 tablespoon chopped onion

1 teaspoon lemon juice
1 tablespoon sugar
½ teaspoon salt
1 cup thick mayonnaise

Mix the ingredients as given and serve cold. This is a favorite dressing for fried fish, soft-shelled crabs, and certain salads.

CUCUMBER SAUCE

1 medium sized fresh cucumber
1 small pickled cucumber
⅛ teaspoon white pepper

1 teaspoon salt
2 tablespoons white vinegar

Pare and grate the cucumbers, mix well with vinegar and seasonings. To be used with fried, boiled or broiled fish.

WHITE SAUCE

A. Thin
1 tablespoon flour
1 tablespoon butter
1 cup milk
¼ teaspoon salt
⅛ teaspoon pepper

B. Medium
2 tablespoons flour
2 tablespoons butter
1 cup milk
¼ teaspoon salt
⅛ teaspoon pepper

C. Thick
4 tablespoons flour
4 tablespoons butter
1 cup milk
¼ teaspoon salt
⅛ teaspoon pepper

Melt the butter, add the flour and cook until it bubbles, then add hot milk. Stir constantly while cooking until the sauce thickens.

LENA'S RED SAUCE

1 cup hot milk
½ cup finely chopped pimento
1 tablespoon lemon juice
2 tablespoons sherry
Yolks of 2 eggs
2 tablespoons flour
1 teaspoon paprika
3 tablespoons butter
Salt, Tabasco and pepper to taste

Melt butter in sauce pan, add flour. Pour in milk slowly, stirring constantly. Add pimento. Let cook over double boiler for 10 minutes. When ready to serve, add well beaten yolks of eggs, lemon juice, seasonings and sherry. Cook for 3 minutes longer.

FRESH MUSHROOM SAUCE

1 pound fresh mushroom
4 tablespoons butter
2 tablespoons lemon juice
1 teaspoon vinegar
1 tablespoon flour
⅛ teaspoon finely chopped garlic
½ teaspoon Worcestershire sauce
Few drops Tabasco
Salt and pepper to taste

Cut stems off mushrooms and wash well in cold water. Place in saucepan with butter and let cook for 15 minutes uncovered.

Then add flour and all seasonings. Let cook for 3 minutes longer and serve over meat.

Canned mushrooms can be substituted for the fresh, adding ½ cup mushroom water.

HOLLANDAISE SAUCE

2 egg yolks
½ teaspoon salt
⅛ teaspoon cayenne pepper

½ cup melted butter
1 tablespoon lemon juice

Beat egg yolks until thick. Add salt, cayenne and 3 tablespoons of the melted butter, a drop at a time. Beat the rest of the butter and the lemon juice alternately. Cook in double boiler stirring continuously until thickened.

STUFFINGS

OYSTER STUFFING

1 cup stale bread
1 tablespoon chopped onion
¼ teaspoon chopped garlic
1 sprig thyme
¼ teaspoon powdered sage
1 bay leaf

1 tablespoon chopped bacon
1 dozen small oysters
½ cup butter or shortening
2 tablespoons water or oyster liquor
Pepper and salt to taste

Mix all ingredients and add melted butter and enough water or oyster liquor so mixture will hold together.

This is a standard stuffing for any sort of fowl or meat. The same amount of Corn Bread (page 25) or cooked rice may be substituted for the stale bread and so vary the stuffing.

BREAD STUFFING

Refer to STUFFED PORK CHOPS recipe.

RICE STUFFING

6 slices fried chopped bacon
2 tablespoons chopped garlic
½ teaspoon chopped garlic
2 tablespoons chopped green pepper
1 dozen chopped oysters
1½ cups dry cooked rice
½ cup oyster water or ordinary water

3 tablespoons shortening
2 tablespoons butter
1 tablespoon chopped celery
2 tablespoons chopped parsley
¼ teaspoon cayenne pepper
Salt and pepper to taste

Mix all ingredients together, except water and rice. Fry in shortening and butter. Add water and rice, stir well then add seasonings.

This dressing can be used for stuffing meat, game or fowl. Giblets can be added, if desired.

COMPOTES

ORANGE COMPOTE

6 medium sized oranges	2 cups sugar
1 quart water	4 slices lemon

Wash oranges and pierce with a fork about eight times. Place in a pot with water, cover and boil until skins are tender. Remove from fire, drain and cool. Cut oranges in half and remove seeds with fork. Place back in the pot with 2 cups sugar, 1 cup water, 4 slices lemon, and let cook ten minutes.

Serve this compote as above, or stuff with cherry apples or mashed sweet potatoes.

CHERRY APPLES COMPOTE

6 medium sized firm apples	4 slices lemon
1 cup sugar	¼ teaspoon red vegetable coloring
2 cups water	

Boil together sugar, coloring, lemon and water for about seven minutes. While boiling, peel and scoop apples with a round potato cutter. Boil apple rounds in liquid about 16 minutes. Let cool to serve. If a large quantity is to be made, scoop apple rounds and cover with cold water to prevent discoloration.

PEAR COMPOTE

4 pears	2 sups sugar
2 cups water	½ lemon

Cook sugar and ½ lemon sliced in water for ten minutes or until thickened. Peel and core pears, cut in half, leaving stems on. Cook for ten minutes in syrup. Let cool. Roll in pecan crumbs, finely chopped.

CANDIED CARROTS

2 bunches carrots
1 cup sugar
6 slices lemon

½ teaspoon nutmeg
2 cups water

Wash and peepl carrots, dice or cut in shoe-string style. Put in sauce pan with sugar, water, nutmeg and lemon and let cook for 15 to 20 minutes. Serve as a compote with meats or fowl.

BAKED PLANTAINS

3 ripe and soft plantains
½ cup sugar
6 tablespoons butter

1 teaspoon cinnamon
¼ cup water

Peel and cut plantains across in 3 parts and slice lengthwise. Put in a baking dish, add water, sprinkle with sugar and cinnamon. Dot with butter. Bake for 15 to 20 minutes in 350° oven. Serve as a compote.

If plantains are not soft, add a little more water and cook a little longer.

SCALLOPED SWEET POTATOES AND PINEAPPLE

6 medium-sized sweet potatoes
¾ cup pineapple juice
6 small slices pineapple

½ cup brown sugar
¼ cup butter or oil

Parboil potatoes. When cooled, slice potatoes and cut pineapple into small pieces. Arrange alternate layers of sweet potatoes and pineapple in baking dish, so there are only four layers in all. Heat the pineapple juice, brown sugar and butter together. Boil for 3 minutes and pour over sweet potatoes and pineapple. Bake in moderate over for 30 minutes. Serves 8.

[74]

SWEET POTATO SURPRISE

2 cups mashed sweet potatoes   ⅛ teaspoon pepper
1 egg   8 marshmallows
½ teaspoon salt   ½ cup crushed cornflakes

Boil and peel potatoes. Mash or put through ricer. When partly cool, add beaten egg, salt and pepper. If mixture is too dry add a little milk. With floured hands form into 8 round balls with marshmallows hidden inside. Roll in cornflakes, finely crushed. Fry in deep fat hot enough to brown the balls in a few minutes. Fry until brown, drain on absorbent paper.

VEGETABLES

SPINACH SOUFFLE

6 eggs
1 pint milk
2 tablespoons butter
1 cup cooked spinach
3 tablespoons flour

¼ cup grated cheese
½ teaspoon cream of tartar
½ teaspoon salt
Pinch white pepper

Mash spinach through sieve. Separate eggs, beat yolks, and add salt, pepper and flour. Pour milk into saucepan and heat to boiling point. Then pour in yolks and stir until thick. Remove from fire, add butter, spinach and cheese. Set aside to cool. Beat whites of eggs until they begin to foam. Add cream of tartar, and continue to beat until stiff and dry. Fold spinach mixture into whites very lightly, pour into buttered Pyrex dish and bake in moderate oven 35-40 minutes. Serve immediately, not allowing to stand after removing from oven.

STRING BEANS AND SHOE-STRING CARROTS

2 pounds string beans
½ teaspoon cooking soda

5 cups boiling water
Salt and pepper to taste

Prepare beans by cutting strings off sides and soak in cool water for about an hour. Bring 5 cups of water to a boil and add soda. Cook the beans in this water for 20 minutes. Drain off water season with salt and pepper.

6 large carrots
5 cups boiling water

Salt and pepper to taste

Peel carrots and cut shoe-string style. Cook in boiling water for twenty minutes. Drain and season with salt and pepper.

Place beans in center of platter with carrots around them. Pour melted butter over all and serve.

STUFFED ARTICHOKES

Boil artichokes and keep hot. Remove inner leaves and choke. Fill artichoke cups with stuffing of Creamed Mushrooms, Creamed Sweetbreads or Seafood Poulet Sauce. Garnish with parsley and serve.

FRIED TOMATOES

6 tomatoes	Bread crumbs
1 egg	Salt and pepper

Use firm ripe tomatoes. Wash and cut in slices about ½ inch thick. Season the bread crumbs with the salt and pepper. Dip the tomatoes in well-beaten egg and then in the crumbs. Fry in hot shortening or cooking oil.

PANEE CAULIFLOWER

1 medium-sized cauliflower	½ cup flour
2 eggs	½ cup cracker meal
4 tablespoons light cream	Salt and pepper to taste

Boil cauliflower 10 minutes, remove from fire and drain. When cool divide into sections. Dip into egg wash (page 135), roll in cracker meal and flour, fry in deep fat and serve immediately.

HASHED BROWN POTATOES

2 tablespoons cooking oil	Salt and pepper
6 boiled potatoes	

Remove skins and chop the potatoes, adding salt and a dash of pepper. Heat fat in frying pan and add the potatoes to the

[77]

depth of one inch. Press the potatoes down into the pan, packing them firmly. Cook slowly, without stirring, until the potatoes are brown. Then begin at one side of the pan and fold the potatoes over on the other, like an omelet, packing closely together.

BAKED POTATOES

Scrub skins of medium-sized Irish or sweet potatoes. Grease well with cooking oil. Bake in moderate oven from 35 to 40 minutes. Large potatoes require an hour to bake.

SMOTHERED CABBAGE

1 three or four pound cabbage	1 pod garlic
½ pound pickled meat	4 tablespoons shortening
1 medium size onion	Salt and pepper to taste

Wash and cut cabbage in coarse pieces. Fry meat in shortening until light brown. Add cabbage and water, onion and garlic. Let cook for 25 minutes. Season with salt and pepper to taste. Serve with Corn Bread (page 25) or Rice.

CAULIFLOWER BALLS

2 cups boiled mashed cauliflower	1 teaspoon baking powder
½ cup American cheese	½ teaspoon salt
2 eggs	¼ teaspoon white pepper
1½ cups cracker meal	

Mix cauliflower with ¾ cup of cracker meal and all ingredients. Shape into round balls. Roll in remaining cracker meal. Fry in deep fat until light brown.

CREAMED SPINACH

4 bunches spinach	½ teaspoon vinegar
½ teaspoon cooking soda	¾ cup milk
1 quart water	Salt and pepper to taste
2 tablespoons flour	

Prepare spinach. Add soda to boiling water and cook for 7 minutes. Remove from fire and strain and press through sieve or ricer. Blend butter, flour and milk together. Add spinach, salt, pepper and vinegar. Cook again for about 3 minutes. Serve on thin buttered toast with hard chopped eggs.

CREAMED ASPARAGUS PLAIN OR WITH CHEESE

1 can asparagus
4 slices hot buttered toast
3 tablespoons butter
4 tablespoons flour
1½ cups milk

½ teaspoon salt
¼ teaspoon paprika
1 teaspoon chopped onion
¼ teaspoon celery salt

Make White Sauce (page 70), add seasonings and cook slowly, stirring constantly. Arrange the asparagus on buttered toast and pour the sauce over them. Serve at once. This same sauce can be made by adding one-fourth cup of grated cheese to it.

SPINACH MOUSSE

2 cups spinach (passed through colander)
3 eggs
¼ cup light cream

¼ cup butter
1½ cups bread crumbs
¼ teaspoon pepper
1 teaspoon salt

Mix ingredients in order given, place in a buttered ring-mold, steam for one hour. Remove from mold and fill center with creamed eggs, mushrooms or creamed carrots.

STUFFED GREEN PEPPERS

6 green peppers
1 cup cooked rice
1 tablespoon chopped onion
1 tablespoon chopped parsley

2 small tomatoes
2 tablespoons grated American cheese
Salt and pepper to taste

Wash peppers, remove tops, seeds and membrane. Cut tomatoes in small pieces. Combine other ingredients and seasonings, and stuff peppers with mixture. Set in pan of cold water reaching half-way up sides of peppers. Bake in moderate oven for 45 minutes.

STUFFED BAKED TOMATOES

6 medium sized tomatoes
½ cup soft bread crumbs
1 tablespoon chopped onion
2 tablespoons finely chopped celery

½ cup cooked and chopped meat or shrimp
2 tablespoons melted butter or substitute
Salt and pepper to taste

Wash but do not peel the tomatoes. Cut slice from stem end of each tomato and scoop out centers. Mix centers with other ingredients. Sprinkle inner sides of tomatoes with salt and fill with the mixture. Top with dried crumbs and dot with butter. Place in a shallow greased pan and bake in a moderate oven 350°, from twenty to twenty-five minutes.

CREAMED TURNIPS

6 white turnips
Juice of 1 lemon
2 eggs
2 tablespoons flour

1½ cups milk
1 teaspoon salt
¼ teaspoon pepper
1 teaspoon paprika

Pare 6 white turnips and dice them. Cook 15 minutes in boiling water to which the lemon juice has been added to make it rather acid. Drain and set away to cool. Mash the yolks of 2 hard-boiled eggs and blend with flour. Then add warm milk gradually, and cook over hot water until thick. Add seasonings. Add the diced turnips and simmer for a few minutes. Remove from fire and add a teaspoon of lemon juice.
Serve at once.

CARROTS A LA KING

6 cups diced carrots
2 cups medium white sauce
1 tablespoon finely chopped celery
1 teaspoon finely chopped onion

1 tablespoon finely chopped parsley
1 tablespoon finely chopped pimento

Cook carrots until tender and drain off water. To white sauce add seasonings. Pour over carrots and serve.

CREOLE COOKED RED BEANS

2 cups Red Beans
1 large onion
½ pound pickled meat or ham shank
3 pods garlic
1 green pepper

2 tablespoons chopped parsley
1 bay leaf
3 tablespoons shortening
2½ quarts of water
Salt and pepper to taste

Soak beans over night. Cook with seasonings, meat and shortening until creamy, except parsley. Just before ready to serve add parsley and salt and pepper to taste.

BOILED GREEN CORN

Remove the husks from the ears of corn. Plunge them into boiling water and cook from seven to twelve minutes. Do not salt the cooking water as this toughens the corn. Drain, sprinkle with salt, place on platter, and serve with drawn butter sauce.

SUCCOTASH

1 pint shelled lima beans
8 ears green corn
1 cup milk

2 tablespoons butter
Salt and pepper to taste

Boil the lima beans until tender in two cups of water. Add salt and pepper to the beans. Cut the corn from the cob and scrape remaining kernels. Add the milk, butter, salt and pepper to the corn and cook a few minutes. Drain water from the beans, and mix with corn. Cook five minutes longer, then serve.

CORN PUDDING

2 cups canned corn or fresh corn
1 cup corn meal
5 eggs
¼ pound butter

1 quart milk
4 tablespoons sugar
1 teaspoon salt
5 teaspoons baking powder

Cream butter, sugar and salt. Add corn, cornmeal, eggs and baking powder. Stir well, add milk and bake in a buttered pyrex dish or casserole in moderate oven for 45 to 50 minutes

LENA'S STUFFED TOMATOES

6 tomatoes (firm and smooth)
1½ cups soft bread crumbs
¼ teaspoon pepper

2 tablespoons shortening
1 teaspoon salt
1 cup cooked shrimp

Tomatoes of equal size should be used. Cut a piece from the stem end of each tomato, and remove the centers without breaking. Make a stuffing of the centers, crumbs, seasoning and melted fat. Cook until done. Stuff the tomatoes with this, sprinkle with bread crumbs and cook in a hot oven ten minutes. Serve immediately.

FRIED ONION RINGS No. 1

2 large white onions cut in rings
1 egg
½ cup flour
½ cup cracker crumbs

¼ cup milk
1 teaspoon salt
¼ teaspoon white or black pepper

Mix beaten egg, milk, salt and pepper. Add onion rings and soak one-half hour. Mix flour and cracker crumbs, dip onions in same, fry in deep fat and drain on brown paper to absorb grease.

Eggplant sliced can replace onions in recipe.

MUSHROOMS

To prepare mushrooms for cooking by any method, cut off the stalks, brush well if they are fresh and tender; if not then pare the caps. Drop them into a bowl of water which contains the juice of half a lemon or a tablespoon of vinegar, if you wish to keep them from darkening. If the stalks are solid and tender, they may be peeled, cooked and served with the caps; otherwise cook them with the peelings in a small amount of water for mushroom stock.

Too much cooking toughens mushrooms. Three or four minutes will heat canned mushrooms, and five or six minutes will usually cook fresh ones.

TEN-MINUTE BOILED CABBAGE WITH MELTED BUTTER OR CREAMED SAUCE

1 head of cabbage
Melted butter *or*

White sauce
Water

Remove the outer leaves from the head of cabbage. Cut it into slices across the leaves so that it will fall in shreds. Put into boiling water and boil ten minutes. Remove from fire and drain. Serve with melted butter or cream sauce.

BOILED ARTICHOKES

Artichokes
1 lemon, cut in halves

Hollandaise Sauce *or*
French Dressing

Cut off stems of the artichokes close to leaves and trim by cutting one inch from top of leaves. Soak for ½ hour in cold water and drain. Bring water to boiling point, squeeze lemon juice into water and add rinds. Boil for 30 to 45 minutes, place upside down and drain again. When cold, serve with Hollandaise Sauce or French Dressing in individual containers on large plates. Boiled artichokes may be served hot with drawn butter sauce, in small containers.

BAKED ARTICHOKES

6 artichokes
1 dozen chopped oysters
½ cup ground raw veal
2 tablespoons chopped green pepper
1 chopped medium-sized onion

1 finely chopped small piece of garlic
½ cup cooking oil
½ cup bread crumbs
½ cup water
Salt and pepper to taste

Prepare artichokes by boiling only 20 to 25 minutes. Drain, cool, remove inner leaves and choke. Set artichokes aside. Heat oil in frying pan, add all ingredients and cook five minutes. Fill artichoke cups with stuffing and place in baking pan with 1 cup of water and bake 20 minutes in a 350° oven. Serve hot.

BROCCOLI

Trim off and discard the leaves and tough lower portion of the stalks of broccoli. Thoroughly wash the remaining center stalks with flower heads attached, and cut lengthwise into strips. Wrap in cheesecloth with flower tops up. Drop into boiling water, leave the pot uncovered, and cook for 15 to 25 minutes. As soon as the broccoli is tender, and while the color is still fresh green, drain, season with salt and pepper to taste, and add melted butter, or serve with Hollandaise sauce. Broccoli can be retained green by addition of ½ teaspoon of cooking soda.

FRIED ONION RING No. 2

4 large white onions cut in rings
1 egg
1 cup flour
½ cup water

1 teaspoon baking powder
¼ teaspoon white or black pepper
1 teaspoon salt

Beat egg, add to flour, salt, pepper and baking powder. Add water slowly and beat until smooth. Dip onions in batter. Fry in deep fat until brown. Drain and serve immediately.

BAKED MIRLETONS (VEGETABLE PEARS)

4 mirletons
2 tablespoons cooking oil
2 tablespoons butter
2 tablespoons chopped onion
1 tablespoon chopped green pepper

1 tablespoon chopped celery
1 tablespoon chopped parsley
¼ cup bread crumbs
1 teaspoon lemon juice
Salt and pepper to taste

Cut pears in half. Cook about 25 minutes in unsalted water. Drain off water, let pears cool. Prepare stuffing by first frying onions, green pepper and celery in cooking oil. Scoop out skins of mirletons. Set aside to stuff. Mix together pear pulp, bread crumbs, melted butter, parsley, lemon etc. Cook a few minutes. Stuff skins. Sprinkle with bread crumbs. Let brown in oven.

SHOE-STRING POTATOES

Wash and peel several fairly large potatoes, in order to get a shoe-string effect. Cut into thin long strips about the size of a shoe string. Soak in cold water for at least 30 minutes or more. Drain and dry in a clean cloth. Put in deep medium hot fat, place on absorbent paper and sprinkle with salt and pepper. When ready to serve put potatoes back in deep hot fat and fry, at least, one or two minutes.

POTATO PUFFS

6 medium sized potatoes	2 teaspoons baking powder
4 tablespoons butter	½ teaspoon white pepper
1 egg	2 teaspoons salt
½ cup milk	

Mash potatoes well. Add milk, egg, butter and baking powder. Stir well. Season with salt and pepper. Drop by large spoonfuls on a well-greased sheet pan and bake from 10 to 15 minutes in the upper part of the oven. Potato puffs can be made very attractive by pressing through a pastry bag.

MACARONI, RICE, CHEESE

MACARONI AND CHEESE

1 cup macaroni	½ cup grated cheese
2 cups milk	2 tablespoons flour
½ teaspoon salt	

Cook macaroni in boiling salted water 20 minutes. Drain. Mix flour and salt with grated cheese. Put layer of macaroni in a buttered baking dish. Cover with cheese mixture, repeat layers, having cheese on top. Pour over all just enough milk to cover top layer. Bake 45 minutes in a moderate oven.

JUMBALAYA

2 cups rice	1 sprig thyme
1 cup canned tomatoes	1 bay leaf
1 medium size slice raw ham	1 cup shrimp
1 large onion	½ cup shortening
1 green pepper	Salt and pepper to taste
2 pods garlic	2 cups water

Wash rice until clear, at least four times. Fry with shortening and onion until brown. Add the meat, shrimp, tomatoes and the rest of the seasoning. Let cook on very slow fire from 30-35 minutes. Crab, oysters, chicken or brisket may be added if desired.

FRIED GRITS

1 cup white or yellow grits	2 eggs
2 cups water	½ cup cracker crumbs or corn
1 teaspoon salt	meal

Boil grits in salted water for fifteen minutes. Pour and spread in a buttered dish. Let stand until thoroughly cold, then cut into squares of three inches. Beat eggs, add milk and season well with salt and pepper. Dip squares in this egg wash and then dip in cracker crumbs. Fry in deep hot fat.

BOILED RICE

1 cup rice	1 tablespoon salt
4 cups water	

Wash rice and rub well between hands. Drop into salted boiling water and boil rapidly, uncovered, for fifteen to twenty minutes until kernels are cooked through. Put rice in a colander and pour boiling water over it to remove loose starch and separate grains. Drain well and place in slow oven with the door open until grains are thoroughly separated and dry, or about twenty minutes.

SLOW-COOKED RICE

1 cup rice	½ teaspoon salt
1½ cups water	

Wash rice by rubbing between the hands, four or five times. Add cold water to rice, let come to a boil then reduce heat, until the water just barely bubbles. Place asbestos pad under sauce pan to prevent burning. In about 40 minutes, the water should be absorbed by the rice. Let it dry out for about 10 minutes and serve.

MACARONI

1 cup of macaroni (broken in small pieces)	1 teaspoon finely chopped onions
1 cup cream	1 teaspoon salt
1 cup bread crumbs	½ cup butter (melted)
1 cup pimento (chopped)	3 eggs (beaten separately)
1 tablespoon chopped parsley	

Cook macaroni in boiling salted water, blanch and drain. Pour milk over bread crumbs and melted butter, add egg yolks, macaroni, and all other ingredients. Fold well beaten whites of eggs, to the mixture, put in well greased ring mold. Stand in hot water and bake in oven 450° F. Bake 45 to 50 minutes. In center of mold serve with mushroom sauce or tomato sauce.

WELSH RAREBIT No. 1

½ pound yellow cheese, shredded thin
1 pint milk
4 tablespoons flour
4 tablespoons melted butter
½ teaspoon mustard
½ teaspoon salt
1 egg
Few drops Tabasco, Worcestershire sauce and onion juice

Heat milk in double-boiler. Mix melted butter, flour, and salt, and smooth with a small amount of milk. Add this to the remainder of milk and stir until thickened, then add the cheese and seasonings. Beat until the cheese has melted. Pour a little of this mixture into the well-beaten egg, then mix all together. Cook 2 or 3 minutes longer. Serve on crisp crackers of toast.

PUDDINGS AND SAUCES

DATE AND NUT PUDDING

1 cup sugar	1 teaspoon baking powder
2 eggs	1 cup chopped dates
2 tablespoons milk	1 cup chopped nuts
2 tablespoons flour	

Separate yolks from whites of eggs. Beat yolks until light and stir in sugar and milk. Sift flour and baking powder together and add to mixture. Then add dates, nuts and stiffly beaten egg whites. Bake in well-greased square pan in moderate oven (350°) for twenty minutes. Serve cold, cut in squares, topped with whipped cream.

UPSIDE DOWN CAKE

For apple cake use 2 firm apples sliced	Pineapple—1 cup crushed or six slices of canned pineapple
Apricots—1 cup drained fruit	3 tablespoons butter
Prunes—½ pound cooked prunes, remove stones	1 cup brown sugar

Drain the fruit. Melt butter and sugar, add the drained fruit and ½ cup chopped nuts. Mix and pour in baking dish. (Make a cake batter as follows)

1 beaten egg	½ cup milk
1 cup sugar	1 cup flour
Pinch salt	1½ teaspoon baking powder
1 teaspoon vanilla	

Pour over fruits and bake in a baking dish 35-40 minutes in a moderate oven. Serve with whipped cream.

LENA'S BAKED CUSTARD

2 eggs
2 tablespoons sugar
2 cups milk

1 teaspoon vanilla
Pinch salt

Break eggs into a bowl, add sugar and beat with a spoon, pour in milk, add salt. Stir and strain through a fine sieve. Add vanilla, stir again and pour into custard cups. Place the cups in a shallow pan containing one and one-half inches of hot water and place in oven. The water in the bottom of the baking pan should not boil. After custard has baked about ½ hour insert a silver knife in the center of each cup. If the knife comes out clear, the custard is done; if it comes out coated, the custard is not done. When cooked allow to cool before serving.

MERINGUES

4 egg whites
1 teaspoon cream tartar

1 teaspoon vanilla extract
3 cups confectioner's sugar

Beat egg whites until they begin to foam, add cream tartar and continue to beat until stiff and dry. Add confectioner's sugar until whites stand stiffly, then add vanilla extract. Line pan with buttered paper, drop large tablespoonfuls into the pan. Bake in a very slow oven until dry. If necessary turn off oven and continue to dry in hot oven.

This meringue squeezed from a pastry bag make lovely shells in which ice cream or fruit may be served.

If the eggs are extra large more sugar may be added; this prevents the meringue from running.

LENA'S APPLE BREAD PUDDING

8 slices stale or dry bread
2 large apples *or*
3 small apples
1 cup raisins
1 cup sugar
4 eggs

½ cup melted butter
1 quart milk
1 teaspoon nutmeg
1 teaspoon vanilla
¼ teaspoon cream of tartar

[90]

Separate 3 eggs leaving the whites for meringue. Beat the yolks of 3 eggs and the whole egg together until light. Add sugar, beat again. Add melted butter, nutmeg, vanilla, milk. Line pan with 4 slices of bread, add a layer of raisins and sliced apples; another layer of bread and the remainder of raisins and apples. Pour first mixture over this. Bake in a moderate oven for 30 minutes. Remove from oven and make meringue with 4 tablespoons Confectioner's sugar folded into stiffly beaten egg whites with ¼ teaspoon cream of tartar. Spread over pudding and put back in oven to brown.

BREAD PUDDING

3 eggs	4 tablespoons butter
2 cups bread crumbs	1 quart milk
½ teaspoon cinnamon	½ teaspoon salt
½ cup raisins	½ teaspoon nutmeg

Melt butter in scalded milk and add bread crumbs. Beat eggs until light and add salt, spices, eggs and raisins to bread mixture. Pour in buttered baking dish and place dish in a shallow pan with about 1½ inches of water in it. Bake in a moderate oven about an hour. Serve warm with Hard Sauce or Hot Lemon Sauce (page 94).

SOUFFLE CREAM PUDDING

4 eggs	2 tablespoons butter
½ cup sugar	1 teaspoon vanilla
4 tablespoons flour	½ teaspoon cream tartar
1 pint milk	

Separate eggs, beat yolks until light. Add sugar and flour and beat again for a few minutes. Heat milk to boiling point. Pour into milk the first mixture and cook until thick, about 3 minutes. Remove from fire, add butter and let cool. Beat egg whites until it begins to foam. Add cream of tartar and continue to beat until stiff. Then fold into first mixture. Pour into well-buttered pyrex dish. Cook in pan of water in moderate oven 35 minutes. Serve immediately.

SWEET POTATO PUDDING

3 sweet potatoes of medium size	¼ teaspoon grated nutmeg
2 eggs well beaten	½ cup brown sugar
1/3 teaspoon salt	2 cups milk

Boil potatoes until soft, mash thoroughly, and mix with all other ingredients. Pour into buttered baking dish and bake in 250° oven until firm. Cover with meringue or marshmallows, if desired, and brown under flame.

Sweet potato pudding is a dish to be served hot as a vegetable with the dinner and not as a dessert. However, this same recipe is also delicious used as a filling for pie.

OLD-FASHIONED GOLDEN BROWN SAUCE

¼ cup brown sugar, firmly packed	1 egg white, beaten
1 egg yolk, unbeaten	¼ cup cream, whipped
Pinch of salt	½ teaspoon vanilla

Sift sugar, add one half of sugar to egg yolk and beat until light. Add salt to egg white and beat until foamy. Add remaining sugar, 1 tablespoon at a time, beating after each addition until sugar is blended. Beat until stiff. Combine egg yolk and egg white mixtures. Fold in whipped cream and vanilla. Serve cold.

WHIPPING CREAM SAUCE

1 egg white	½ cup whipping cream
1 tablespoon sugar	¼ teaspoon vanilla

Whip egg white and cream separately, until very stiff. Sweeten cream and flavor with vanilla or any flavor desired. Fold whipped cream into egg whites.

CRANBERRY SAUCE

2 cups cranberries   ½ cup water
1 cup sugar

Pick over and wash the cranberries. Boil cranberries in water until the skins burst. Press through a sieve then add sugar. Let cook for 10 minutes. Overcooked cranberries are bitter.

CHOCOLATE SAUCE

1 cup sugar   ¾ teaspoon vanilla
4 tablespoons cocoa   ½ cup milk
1 tablespoon butter

Put sugar, cocoa, milk in a sauce pan. Boil until it forms a very soft ball in cold water. Add butter and vanilla and allow to cool.

HARD SAUCE

4 tablespoons butter   1¼ cups confectioner's sugar
2 tablespoons rum, sherry, brandy or whiskey

Cream butter and add sugar gradually until it all has blended in. Then add flavoring.

HOT BUTTERSCOTCH SAUCE

1 cup dark corn syrup   ½ cup sugar
1 tablespoon milk   1 tablespoon butter
¼ teaspoon salt   ½ teaspoon vanilla

Bring to a boil the syrup, sugar and milk; stirring constantly 5 minutes. Continue boiling without stirring until a little of the syrup forms a soft ball in cold water. Remove from fire, add butter, salt and vanilla. Stir until blended. Add enough boiling water to give syrup desired pouring consistency, approximately two tablespoons.

CREAM FILLING

1 cup milk	½ cup sugar
2 eggs	½ teaspoon vanilla
1 tablespoon cornstarch	

Beat whole eggs until light. Add sugar and cornstarch. Pour into boiling milk, let cook for 3 minutes in double boiler. Remove from fire. When cool, add vanilla.

HOT LEMON SAUCE

1½ tablespoons cornstarch	1 tablespoon butter
½ cup sugar	1 cup boiling water
Grated rind of ½ lemon	1 tablespoon lemon juice

Mix together cornstarch and sugar. Add boiling water slowly, place in top of double boiler and cook 15 minutes over the boiling water, stirring constantly until smooth and thickened. Remove from heat, add butter, grated rind and lemon juice. Serve hot over Bread Pudding or left-over slices of cake.

SHERRY SAUCE

½ cup milk	4 tablespoons butter
1 cup sugar	2 tablespoons sherry

Boil milk, sugar and butter together for five minutes. Add sherry.

This sauce is delicious over Souffle Cream Pudding (page 91), stale cake, Apple Dumplings (page 97), etc.

DESSERTS

LEMON DELIGHT

1 cup sugar	Rind of 2 lemons
1 pint milk	¾ cup graham crackers
3 tablespoons Knox gelatine	4 eggs
Juice of 3 lemons	

Separate eggs. Beat yolks until light. Add sugar. Heat milk to a boiling point and add to the above mixture. Add gelatine then add lemon juice and rind. Pour entire mixture into stiffly beaten egg whites then pour into a pan that has been greased with butter and lined with crushed graham crackers, to form a crust. Put in refrigerator to harden. Top with whipped cream passed through a pastry bag. Spring mold pan must be used.

SPANISH CREAM

½ cup cold water	2 tablespoons gelatine
1 pint milk	½ cup sugar
4 eggs	1 teaspoon vanilla

Separate eggs and beat yolks until light. Add sugar and beat again. Heat milk to the boiling point, then stir in egg and sugar mixture and let cook for 3 minutes. Remove from fire and add the gelatine which has been soaked in cold water. When cool, add the stiffly beaten egg whites and vanilla. Put into mold in the ice box until firm.

This dessert may be served with whipped cream.

LEMON AND ORANGE SURPRISE

1 lemon	½ cup milk
1 orange	4 tablespoons butter
2 cups sugar	1½ cups flour
1 cup boiling water	2 teaspoons baking powder
3 egg yolks	¼ teaspoon cream of tartar

Peel the lemon and orange and slice very thin, removing seeds. Put in saucepan, add 1 cup sugar and the water and cook slowly until a thin syrup is formed. Beat yolks of eggs. Add rest of sugar and melted butter. Add sifted baking powder and flour alternately with milk. Pour lemon syrup into a buttered baking dish, pour over batter but do not stir. Bake in 375° oven for 1 hour. When done spread meringue over top and brown. Make meringue by beating the 3 egg whites until it begins to foam, add cream of tartar, continue to beat until stiff and dry then add 4 tablespoons of sugar. Serve hot or cold.

CHOCOLATE ICE BOX CAKE

1 cup confectioner's sugar	½ cup granulated sugar
2/3 cup butter	4 eggs
2 squares bitter chocolate	1 pint heavy cream, whipped
4 tablespoons water	

Melt chocolate in water in a double boiler, add granulated sugar and beaten egg yolks. Cook until it thickens, stirring constantly. Let cool before adding the creamed butter and confectioner's sugar. Lastly, fold in stiffly beaten whites.

If Lady Fingers are used it will take from 2½ to 3 dozen. Line bottom and sides of a mold with the split fingers, pour in filling and put a few split fingers on top. Place in ice box for, at least, twelve hours. When ready to serve, remove rim from pan and place on large cake plate. Top with sweetened and flavored whipped cream. Decorate with cherries and nuts, if desired.

PINEAPPLE ICE BOX CAKE

2 dozen lady fingers or small sponge cake
1 cup diced pineapple
¼ cup blanched almonds
½ cup marshmallows
½ cup whipped cream
¼ cup sugar
1/8 teaspoon salt
½ cup pineapple juice
2 teaspoons lemon juice
1 tablespoon gelatine
1 tablespoon water (cold)

Soak gelatine in cold water. Chop almonds and break marshmallows into small pieces (marshmallows will not stick if you first dip fingers in cold water). Heat pineapple and lemon juices together and mix with dissolved gelatine. Then add ingredients in following order:—whipped cream, sugar, salt, almonds, pineapple and marshmallows. Line mold with lady fingers and proceed as in chocolate ice-box cake.

APPLE DUMPLING

2 medium sized apples
2 cups flour
½ teaspoon salt
½ cup shortening
1 teaspoon baking powder
½ cup butter
1½ cups sugar
2 teaspoons cinnamon or nutmeg

Pare, core and quarter apples. Prepare dough by Baking Powder Biscuit recipe (substitution 7 tablespoons of water for milk and using only 1 teaspoon of baking powder.) and roll on floured board one-fourth inch thick. Cut dough into 8 squares, fill cavity around apple with 1 teaspoon sugar and ¼ teaspoon cinnamon or nutmeg and a dot of butter. Fold dough around and over apple and place dumplings well apart in baking pan, 3 or 4 inches deep. Fill pan with 3 cups of boiling water, remaining sugar and butter, just leaving tops of dumplings uncovered. Bake for 25 minutes in 350° oven. Serve dumplings hot with a sauce made by using part of the liquid in which they have been cooked, mixed with one part of thick cream. Flavor with 2 tablespoons sherry (if desired).

BAKED APPLE

6 large apples
1½ cups sugar
½ teaspoon nutmeg

6 slices lemon
2 cups water

Wash and core apples. Place in a baking pan with sugar, water, nutmeg and lemon. Bake in 350° oven for 35 to 40 minutes. Baste frequently while cooking. Serve plain or with whipping or plain cream.

FLOATING ISLAND

1 pint milk
3 eggs
¾ cup sugar
6 tablespoons confectionery sugar

1 teaspoon vanilla
2 tablespoons flour
½ teaspoon cream tartar

Separate eggs, beat whites until they begin to foam, add cream of tartar, continue to beat until stiff and dry. Add confectioner's sugar and beat. Heat milk to boiling point. Drop egg whites in by large spoonsful about the size of an egg, until all whites have been used. Let cook for a few seconds then turn over. As they cook remove from the milk and set aside. Beat yolks of eggs until light then add sugar and flour and pour into same milk to make a custard and cook from 3 to 5 minutes. When cool add vanilla and serve in individual glasses with meringue on top.

CHARLOTTE RUSSE

1 pint whipping cream
4 egg yolks
2 egg whites
½ cup granulated sugar
½ cup confectionery sugar

½ cup nuts
2 tablespoons gelatine
½ cup cold water
1 teaspoon vanilla extract

Separate eggs. Beat yolks until lemon colored. Add sugar. Cream until light. Add chopped nuts and vanilla. Add gelatine which has been soaked and dissolved in the half cup of water. Whip the cream and add ½ cup of Confectionery sugar, then add egg whites which have been stiffly beaten. Pour into glasses lined with lady fingers. The top can be made fancy with cherries and chopped nuts.

STRAWBERRY SHORTCAKE

2 cups flour	2 tablespoons sugar
2 teaspoons baking powder	1 egg
½ teaspoon salt	3 cups strawberries
½ cup shortening	

Prepare pastry for shortcake by blending shortening in flour with knives or finger tips. Add baking powder, salt and whole egg then 5 tablespoons iced water. Pat the dough out in a well-greased and slightly floured deep pie pan. Bake 20 to 25 minutes in 350° oven. Remove from oven and let cool. Split the shortcake in half.

Crush 2 cups fresh strawberries, sweeten with sugar to taste. Place on bottom half of shortcake. Replace upper half and cover with whipped cream. Garnish with other cup of strawberries.

BAKED PRUNE WHIP

1 cup boiled and pitted prunes	½ teaspoon cream of tartar
3 egg whites	½ teaspoon vanilla
6 tablespoons Confectioner's sugar	

Pass prunes through a sieve. Beat whites until light then add cream of tartar and continue to beat until stiff and dry. Then add sugar, vanilla and fold in the prunes. Pour into a buttered dish and bake in 350° oven for 10 to 15 minutes. When cold serve with whipped cream.

CAKES AND ICINGS

ANGEL FOOD CAKE

10 egg whites
1¼ cups sugar
1 cup flour

½ teaspoon cream of tartar
1 teaspoon almond extract
1 teaspoon lemon juice

Beat whites until foamy then add cream of tartar; beat to stiff frost. Add sugar and beat until sugar is melted. Add lemon juice and flavoring and beat well. Then fold in flour carefully. Bake at 350° in an unbuttered Van Dush Baking Pan, 30 minutes. Remove from oven and reverse pan and let cake remain in this position until cold.

SPONGE CAKE

4 egg yolks
4 egg whites
1 cup pastry flour
1 cup sugar
1¼ tablespoons corn starch

4 tablespoons cold water
1½ teaspoons baking powder
¼ teaspoon salt
1 teaspoon lemon extract

Beat yolks until thick and lemon colored, add sugar gradually, add flavoring and flour sifted with salt, cornstarch and baking powder. Fold in stiffly beaten egg whites and bake in moderate oven 25 to 60 minutes, depending on shape of pan, whether flat or whole cake.

CHOCOLATE FUDGE CAKE

2 cups sifted flour
2 teaspoons baking powder
½ teaspoon salt
½ cup butter
1 cup sugar

2 heaping tablespoons cocoa
1 egg well-beaten
1 teaspoon vanilla
¾ cup milk

Sift flour once, measure, add baking powder and salt, and sift together three times. Cream butter thoroughly, add sugar gradually, and cream together until light and fluffy. Add cocoa and blend. Then add egg and vanilla. Add flour, alternately with milk; a small amount at a time. Beat after each addition until smooth. Bake in a greased pan in moderate 350° oven one hour. Cover cake with fudge frosting.

JELLY ROLLS

¾ cup sugar
3/8 cup hot water
1½ teaspoons baking powder
¼ teaspoon salt
½ teaspoon lemon extract

7/8 cup flour
2 eggs
Small jar jelly
2 tablespoons confectioner's sugar

Beat egg yolks until thick and lemon colored. Add one-half of sugar gradually. Add hot water and then the rest of the sugar. Add lemon extract, and flour sifted with the salt. Fold in stiffly beaten egg whites, and bake on a baking sheet lined with greased paper, in a moderate oven (350°) for 25 minutes. Turn pan out on damp towel, remove paper, cut off edges, spread jelly. Roll and wrap in towel. This has to be done while cake is hot. Let cool in towel then just before serving remove cake from towel and sprinkle with confectioner's sugar.

WHITE SILVER CAKE

1 cup butter
2 cups sugar
1 cup milk
3½ cups flour

1 teaspoon almond extract
4 teaspoons baking powder
7 egg whites

Cream butter until fluffy, add sugar and cream again. Sift flour three times, adding baking powder the third time. Add alternately, a small quantity at a time, milk and flour to the creamed butter and sugar. Add almond extract and then fold unbeaten egg whites into the batter and beat for 3 minutes. Bake in 350° oven until cake shrinks away from side of pan.

This cake may be baked whole or in layers. A Five Egg layer cake may be made by the same method using only five whole eggs.

GOLDEN CAKE

4 tablespoons butter	¼ cup milk
½ cup sugar	⅞ cup flour
Yolks 5 eggs	1½ teaspoons baking powder
1 teaspoon orange extract	

Cream butter, add sugar gradually and beaten yolks of eggs. Eggs should be beaten till thick and lemon colored. Add extract. Mix and sift flour and baking powder, and add alternately with milk to first mixture. Bake in individual cup cake tins or souffle cups in a moderate (350°) oven about 20 minutes.

DATE AND NUT CAKE

1 cup sugar	3 eggs
2 cups flour	¼ teaspoon cloves
1 teaspoon nutmeg	¾ cup milk
½ cup butter	1 teaspoon cinnamon
4 teaspoons baking powder	½ cup finely chopped dates
1 teaspoon ginger	1 cup finely chopped nuts

Cream the sugar and butter, and add eggs. Beat well. Add ½ cup nuts and add dates. Stir until all well blended. Sift dry ingredients with flour. Alternate with milk. Bake in square sheet pan from 15 to 20 minutes in a moderate oven.

ONE EGG CAKE

4 tablespoons butter	2 cups sifted cake flour
1 cup sugar	2 teaspoons baking powder
¾ cup milk	½ teaspoon vanilla
1 egg	½ teaspoon salt

Cream butter and sugar, add whole egg and beat thoroughly. Then add flour which has been sifted with baking powder and salt, 3 times, alternating with milk. Add vanila. Bake in 2 greased cake tins in a moderate oven 15 to 20 minutes.

SUNSHINE CAKE

Whites of 9 eggs
Yolks of 7 eggs
1¼ cups sugar
1 cup flour

½ teaspoon salt
½ teaspoon cream of tartar
1 teaspoon vanilla

Sift sugar and flour each three times and then measure and set aside. Whip whites of eggs until foamy. Add cream of tartar and continue to whip until dry. Add sugar and whip until sugar is melted. Beat yolks until lemon colored and add these to the white and then the vanilla. Finally, fold in flour lightly until well-blended and bake in a Cake pan in a 350° oven for 45 minutes. Turn upside down on rack and let stand until cool. Use flat knife or spatula to remove from pan. Any icing or frosting may be used if desired.

FRUIT CAKE

1 pound dates
1 pound lemon peeling
1 pound orange peeling
3 pounds raisins
2 pounds currants
1 pound butter
1 pound citron
1 pound nuts
1 cup cherries
1 dozen eggs
1 cup syrup
4 cups sugar

½ pound crystallized pineapple
2 tablespoons cinnamon
1 teaspoon cloves
1 tablespoon ginger
1 tablespoon nutmeg
1 tablespoon mace
6 tablespoons cocoa
8 cups flour
3 teaspoons cooking soda (level)
½ cup cherry juice
½ cup water
3 teaspoons baking powder

Soak spices in water and cherry juice 30 minutes. Brown flour light brown. Cut all the fruits in fine pieces and dredge with the flour. Place aside. Cream butter and sugar, add all eggs, cocoa, syrup and stir well. Then add fruit and flour to this mixture, stir until it is all blended. Add soda and spice and liquid, stir well. Pour over batter and stir thoroughly.

This amount will make an average 16 pound fruit cake that can be baked in 2 cakes or various weights allowing 30 minutes to each pound in a very slow oven.

DEVIL'S FOOD CAKE

2 cups sifted cake flour
1 teaspoon soda
½ cup butter
2 cups sifted brown sugar
3 eggs—unbeaten

6 squares unsweetened chocolate (melted)
1 cup sweet milk
1 teaspoon vanilla

Sift flour once, measure, add soda, and sift together three times. Cream butter thoroughly, add sugar gradually, and cream together until light and fluffy. Add eggs, one at a time and beat well. Add chocolate and beat well. Add flour, alternately with milk, a small amount at a time. Beat after each addition until smooth. Add vanilla. Pour into three greased layer cake pans and bake in a moderate oven (325° F.) for thirty minutes. Spread cooked frosting between layers and on top and sides of cake.

BUTTER ICING

Boiling water, milk or cream
½ teaspoon vanilla

2 tablespoons butter
2 cups confectioner's sugar

Cream butter, work in sifted confectioner's sugar and then add enough liquid for consistency to spread. Icing may be colored to any color desired by adding vegetable coloring.

FUDGE FROSTING

2 heaping tablespoons cocoa
2/3 cup cold milk
2 cups sugar
2 tablespoons corn syrup

2 tablespoons butter
1 teaspoon vanilla
Dash of salt

Add cocoa to milk and place over low flame. Cook until mixture is smooth and blended, stirring constantly. Add sugar, salt and syrup and stir until sugar is dissolved and mixture boils. Continue cooking, without stirring, until a small amount of mixture forms a very soft ball in cold water. Remove from fire, add butter and vanilla. Cool to lukewarm. Beat until of right consistency to spread.

UNCOOKED WHITE ICING

2 egg whites
1½ cups confectioner's sugar
¼ teaspoon lemon juice

¼ teaspoon extract, either vanilla lemon or any other flavor

Beat egg whites to a stiff froth, add sugar gradually and beat until well blended. Add the lemon juice and extract. Spread on cake.

COOKIES, DOUGHNUTS
AND SMALL CAKES

SUGAR COOKIES

4 tablespoons butter
4 tablespoons lard
1 cup sugar
3 cups flour
1 egg

1 teaspoon baking powder
1 teaspoon soda
2 tablespoons sour milk
1 teaspoon vanilla

Cream shortening, add sugar, then well-beaten egg. Sift dry ingredients combine with first mixture and add milk only if egg is not large enough to moisten to right consistency for rolling. Put on a slightly floured board, knead slightly. Roll to ¼ inch thickness, then cut with fancy cookie cutter and place on greased baking sheets. Bake in moderate oven for 8 to 10 minutes.

ICE BOX COOKIES

1 cup white sugar
1 cup brown sugar
1 cup shortening
3½ cups flour
2 teaspoons cinnamon

1 cup chopped nuts
3 eggs
1 teaspoon baking powder
1 teaspoon soda

Mix sugar and shortening with fingers. Add eggs, sifted dry ingredients and nuts. Shape in loaf rolled and put in ice box a few hours. Slice and bake in a 350° oven. Roll may be left in ice box 2 or 3 days to slice and bake when cookies are desired.

OATMEAL COOKIES

¾ cup shortening
1 cup sugar
1 teaspoon cinnamon
¼ teaspoon cloves
½ teaspoon nutmeg
1 egg

2/3 cup coarse oatmeal
2 cups flour
2 teaspoons baking powder
¼ teaspoon soda
1 cup raisins
Pinch of salt

Cream the shortening and add the sugar gradually. Mix well with spices, salt, slightly beaten egg, sour milk and oatmeal. Sift flour, baking powder, soda together, and then add raisins. Combine the two mixtures. Stir well and drop from a spoon on a well-greased pan and bake for 8 to 10 minutes in a moderate (350°) oven.

SLICED NUT COOKIES

1 cup brown sugar
1 cup white sugar
1½ cups melted butter or substitute
3 eggs, well beaten
1 teaspoon salt

5 cups flour
1 teaspoon soda
1 teaspoon cinnamon or other spice
1 cup chopped nuts

Blend butter with sugar. Add eggs slowly, mixing thoroughly. Stir in nuts, then dry ingredients sifted together twice. Shape into roll about two and one half to three inches in diameter. Put in greased pan in ice box over night. When ready to bake, slice thin and bake in moderately hot oven (375° F.)

DOUGHNUTS

2 cups sifted flour
2 teaspoons baking powder
¼ teaspoon salt
½ teaspoon nutmeg
½ teaspoon cinnamon

½ cup sugar
1 egg, well beaten
1 tablespoon butter or other shortening melted
½ cup milk

Sift flour once, measure, add baking powder, salt, nutmeg and cinnamon. Sift together, three times. Combine sugar and egg; add shortening. Add flour, alternately with milk, a small amount at a time. Beat after each addition until smooth. Knead lightly 2 minutes on slightly floured board. Roll 1/3 inch thick. Cut with doughnut cutter. Let rise for several minutes. Fry in deep fat, until a golden brown. Drain on unglazed paper. Sprinkle with powdered sugar, if desired.

DATE BAR

1 cup sugar	1 cup flour
3 eggs	1 tablespoon baking powder
1 cup broken nut meats	¼ teaspoon salt
1 cup dates	

Beat yolks of eggs, add sugar, and cream well. Add salt, nuts, chopped dates, flour and baking powder, and finally well beaten egg whites. Bake on a baking sheet 30 minutes in moderate oven (350°). Cut in strips and roll in powdered sugar.

DATE TART

3 tablespoons cooking oil	1 package dates
1⅓ cups flour	1 cup boiling water
1 teaspoon baking powder	½ teaspoon salt
1 cup walnuts	2 eggs
1 cup sugar	½ teaspoon vanilla

Over the chopped dates, pour the boiling water and allow to stand until cool. Add the cooking oil and eggs which have been beaten together, and the dry ingredients, which have been sifted together. Stir in the nuts and vanilla. Bake on a moderately hot waffle iron for 4 minutes. Serve with hard sauce or whipped cream. This is a delicious dessert for luncheons, dinner or informal supper parties.

PLAIN MUFFINS

2 cups flour	2 eggs
4 teaspoons baking powder	1 cup milk
½ teaspoon salt	3 tablespoons fat
1 to 2 tablespoons sugar	

Beat egg in mixing bowl, add the milk and then the melted fat. Measure the dry ingredients carefully and then add them to the milk and egg mixture. Mix quickly and thoroughly and drop into buttered muffin pans. Bake in a 450° oven from 10 to 15 minutes.

GRAHAM MUFFINS

1 cup Graham flour	2 eggs
2 cups wheat flour	2 tablespoons butter
4 teaspoons baking powder	4 tablespoons sugar
1 cup milk	½ teaspoon salt

Sift all dry ingredients. Cream butter, sugar and eggs. Add alternately with milk to the first mixture. Fill muffin tins to 2/3 full. Bake 20 to 25 minutes in a hot oven 450° F.

CREAM PUFFS

6 tablespoons butter	4 eggs
1 cup boiling water	1 cup flour
½ teaspoon salt	

Place water in saucepan, bring to boiling point, add butter. Stir in quickly the flour sifted with salt. Cook until the mixture forms a mass which clears edge of pan. Remove from fire and let cool 10 minutes. Then beat in eggs, one at a time, blending thoroughly. Drop by the large spoonfuls on greased baking sheet, then reduce the heat to 350°, and continue cooking taking 40 to 45 minutes, or until thoroughly dried out inside. When cool, cut a slit in one side and insert cream filling or whipped cream, flavored to taste with vanilla and powdered sugar. Sprinkle surface with powdered sugar or ice with chocolate icing.

BROWNIES

1 cup sugar	¼ teaspoon baking powder
¾ cup sifted flour	1 cup chopped walnuts or
1½ teaspoons vanilla	pecans
½ cup butter	2 squares melted chocolate
2 eggs	

Cream the butter, add sugar gradually, then the well-beaten eggs and melted chocolate and vanilla. Then add chopped walnut or pecan meats, and flour and baking powder which have been sifted together. Spread evenly in a 10-inch square pan. Bake in a slow oven for 20 minutes. When done, cut in squares. If desired, a fudge icing may be added.

OLD-FASHIONED GINGERBREAD

3 cups flour
2 rolling teaspoons cooking soda
¼ teaspoon salt
½ teaspoon allspice
2 teaspoons cinnamon
2 teaspoons ginger
⅞ cup brown sugar (old-fashioned)

¾ cup butter or shortening
2 eggs
1 cup molasses
1 lemon rind (grated)
Juice of ½ lemon
1 cup buttermilk

Measure three level cupfuls of flour and sift. Sift flour again, this time including all dry ingredients and only one teaspoon soda. Cream well the butter or shortening and brown sugar. Add eggs and beat until light. Add molasses and grated rind of lemon and lemon juice. Then mix in dry ingredients, continuing to beat well. Place teaspoon of soda in buttermilk, stir, and pour into mixture, and beat two minutes. Pour into square pan, which has been greased and floured, and bake 30 minutes in moderate oven.

Rolling teaspoon means more than level but not heaping—heap spoon and then smooth sides.

TEA DAINTIES

7 heaping tablespoons of old Fashioned Brown sugar
½ cup butter

½ cup pecans
18 graham crackers cut in halves

Cream butter and sugar well. Cut graham crackers in half and spread with the mixture. Sprinkle or dip in chopped nuts. Line on greased pan and bake in 350° oven for 10 minutes. Can be made and kept for a long time by putting them in a covered can. The butter and sugar mixture can also be kept in the ice box any length of time.

CHEESE MUFFINS

1 cup sifted flour	2 teaspoons baking powder
3 tablespoons shortening	½ teaspoon salt
½ cup grated cheese	½ cup milk

Sift flour twice with salt and baking powder. Stir in cheese with a fork. Melt shortening and add to milk, then mix with other ingredients. Drop in greased muffin tin. Bake in 450° oven for 15 minutes.

POPOVERS

1 cup flour	2 eggs
¼ teaspoon salt	1 teaspoon shortening
1 cup milk	

Sift flour and salt together. Beat eggs and add the milk and flour alternately, a little at a time, until the whole amount of each is added. Then add melted shortening. Beat entire mixture vigorously with a Dover egg-beater. Pour into greased muffin pan, which has been heated. Bake in hot (400°) oven about 15 minutes or until they have popped. Reduce heat to 350° and continue baking for about 30 minutes. This recipe makes six popovers.

PASTRY AND PIES

PECAN PIE FILLING

1 cup corn syrup	3 eggs
1 cup pecans chopped coarse	1 teaspoon vanilla
½ cup granulated sugar	½ teaspoon salt

Beat eggs slightly, add sugar, syrup and nuts, salt and vanilla.
Put in unbaked shell and bake 30 minutes in a slow oven 350°.
The pecans will float to the top forming a crust that will brown
nicely if baked slowly.

PIE PASTRY

1½ cups flour	¼ teaspoon salt
½ cup shortening	5 tablespoons ice water

Cut shortening into flour with knife or finger tips. Add salt.
Add water slowly, mixing thoroughly. Roll on well-floured
board.

Individual pastry shells can be made by molding over muffin
rings or clam shells. They can be used for individual pies, or
creamed shrimp, oyster, etc.

APPLE PIE FILLING (Large)

4 apples cut in slices and lined around the pie pan	½ teaspoon cinnamon
	½ cup water
1½ cups sugar	13 dots of butter

Slice the apples round. Line the bottom of the pie pan, after
putting in the pastry, with the sliced apple. Sprinkle with sugar
and some of the cinnamon then cover this with more sliced

apple. Sprinkle again with sugar and cinnamon. Continue with these layers until the pan is full. Then pour the water over all and dot with butter. Cover with strips of dough and bake in a moderate oven for at least 30 minutes or until the water has dried and the crust brown.

Use the same Pie Crust recipe given in this book.

LENA'S OLD-FASHIONED CUSTARD PIE

3 eggs
¾ cup sugar
¼ teaspoon salt

2 cups milk
1 teaspoon vanilla

Beat eggs slightly, add sugar, salt and scalded milk slowly. Take off fire and add vanilla. Line pie plate with plain pastry and pour in custard. Bake in 350° oven 25 to 30 minutes. The custard is baked when a knife put in center comes out dry.

LENA'S SINGLE CRUST PIE

For one crust pie in which the crust is to be pre-baked, place the crust on the outside of the pie tin, prick it well with a fork and bake in a hot oven for ten to fifteen minutes. When baked this crust is allowed to cool slightly and then is taken off the bottom of the tin and placed inside it and filled.

MERINGUE FOR LENA'S SINGLE CRUST PIE

From one to two tablespoons Confectioner's sugar to each egg white. Beat white until stiff. Add sugar gradually. Flavor with one-half teaspoon vanilla to two egg whites. Arrange by spoonfuls or with pastry bag on pie. Place in slow oven to brown about five or ten minutes.

TWO CRUST PIE

More pastry is necessary for lower crust than upper. Score upper crust to allow the escape of steam. Moisten under crust with water around edge before placing upper crust on, then press around edge with a fork or fingers. This keeps the two crusts together. If you are making a fruit pie, sprinkle sugar and one or two tablespoons of flour in the bottom of pie to prevent under crust from becoming soggy.

ICE BOX GRAHAM CRACKER LEMON PIE

1 can condensed milk	1 cup Graham cracker crumbs
4 eggs	or Vanilla Wafers
4 tablespoons confectioner's sugar	½ tsp. cream tartar
4 lemons	

Roll cakes very fine and line in well buttered pie pan. Separate eggs, beat yolks until light, add milk, add grated rind of three lemons and juice of 4 lemons. Beat again. Whip whites to stiff froth, add sugar; add 4 heaping teaspoons meringue to lemon custard. Pour over cake crumbs. Add rest of meringue to top of pie

Brown slightly in 450° oven. Remove and cool and then place in refrigerator for four hours or more before serving.

SANDWICHES

White bread, whole wheat, rye or brown bread, crackers, wafers, and quick bread are all suitable for making sandwiches. If bread is cut on a slicer it is more economical than cutting by hand, as the bread can be cut more evenly and thinner. For example, in using a two pound pullman loaf, you can get 30 slices if cut by machine or 25 slices if cut by hand. Thus, a two pound loaf of pullman bread sliced by machine, will make fifteen single sandwiches, which can then be divided into two, three or four depending upon the size sandwich desired.

The bread used for sandwiches should be cut according to the kind of sandwiches to be made. Tea and cocktail sandwiches, hors d'oeuvres, and appetizers, should be dainty and therefore thin slices of fine bread should be selected. Supper or picnic sandwiches should be more filling and therefore, it is not necessary to remove the crust or cut bread thin.

Butter used for spreading on sandwiches should be previously creamed. A mixture of relishes such as, mustard, chives, parsley and pearl onions, mixed with mayonnaise make a delightful spread for all meat sandwiches.

On a whole all sandwiches for formal or informal affairs should be of good content and daintily arranged for serving.

SUGGESTIONS FOR SANDWICHES

All sandwiches should be spread and crust cut from edges, then cut in various shapes, triangles, squares or strips, or fancy cutters.

CLUB SANDWICHES

Cream butter with mayonnaise in equal parts and add small amount finely chopped chow-chow pickle. Spread this on slices of toast allowing three slices for each sandwich. Between each layer place one choice slice of chicken or turkey, one slice bacon, several thin slices of tomato and small leaf of lettuce. Cut sandwich into squares or triangles. Serve with pickles, onions or olives.

ASPARAGUS ROLLED SANDWICH

Cut crust from the desired number of slices of bread. Mix equal parts of mayonnaise and butter. Spread this lightly on bread. In the center and at outer edges of each slice place a small piece of lettuce. Put a half piece of asparagus which has been slightly salted, in the lettuce. Roll this together tightly enough to hold. Keep in ice box in waxed paper or cover with slightly dampened cheese cloth.

This same recipe can be used with cucumbers instead of asparagus.

FANCY SANDWICH

The fancy sandwich is a formula of colored cheeses, highly seasoned, colored, using fancy cutter and decorated open face. Decorate with cake decorator, making fancy designs with cheese or sprinkle cherries, nuts, eggs on top or strips of pimento.

RIBBON SANDWICH

Using sliced bread, sliced on No. 6 Whole Wheat and White bread. Start with a white slice of bread, spread with colored cheese. Over this spread place a brown slice of bread. Spread with the next color cheese. Repeat in same manner until six slices have been used. Wrap in a piece of moistened cloth or wax paper and place in ice box. Cut in ½ inch slices when ready to serve.

CHEESE ROLLS

Cut crust from the desired number of slices of bread. Slices may be left the full length or cut in half if smaller rolls are desired.

CHEESE ROLL MIXTURE

1 cup grated American cheese	¼ teaspoon cayenne pepper
2 tablespoons soft butter	½ teaspoon salt
3 tablespoons mayonnaise	½ teaspoon lemon juice

Cream cheese with all seasonings until creamy. Spread on bread and roll tightly. Toast under flame on both sides. Serve immediately.

SARDINE AND EGG SANDWICH

1 can sardines	¼ teaspoon cayenne pepper
4 hard-boiled eggs	½ teaspoon salt
1 cup mayonnaise	

Mash sardines and chop eggs. Add salt and pepper. Mix and spread between desired number of pieces of sliced bread.

SLICED TURKEY SANDWICH

Use equal parts of butter and mayonnaise, salt and cayenne pepper. Spread slices of bread on both sides. Line with thinly sliced turkey. Cut crust from slices of bread and cut in any shape desired. Sliced ham, sliced tongue or any other sliced meat may be used, likewise. A little mustard may be added to the filling, if desired.

CHICKEN SALAD SANDWICH

2 cups finely chopped chicken	¼ teaspoon cayenne pepper
2 cups mayonnaise	Salt to taste
2 tablespoons butter	
1 tablespoon finely chopped parsley	

Have bread thinly sliced. Mix all ingredients for filling until well-blended. Season to taste. Spread chicken mixture on slice of bread, cover with second slice. Cut crust, from edges, and cut slices in half or smaller, if desired. This recipe can be used for chopped Frankfurters or Weiners, chopped Veal, Turkey, Tuna Fish.

VARIETY OF SANDWICH FILLINGS

1, Minced ham, chopped pickles and mayonnaise.

2. Chopped hard-boiled eggs, chopped crisp fried bacon and mayonnaise.

3. Sliced chicken, ham, sausage, cheese and mayonnaise.

4. Creamed Philadelphia Cheese, chopped nuts and mayonnaise.

5. Jams, jellies, peanut butter and marmalade.

6. Minced salmon, tuna or shrimp, mayonnaise.

7. Anchovy paste, mustard and butter.

8. Roquefort cheese, mayonnaise, Worcestershire sauce.

9. Chopped olives, mayonnaise, salt and pepper.

CANDY

PEANUT CANDY

1 cup sugar
½ cup dark corn syrup
¼ cup water
1 cup raw, shelled and unsalted
  peanuts

1 teaspoon butter
1 teaspoon vanilla
1 teaspoon soda

Boil sugar, syrup and water, until it spins into a thread when tested. Add butter, then peanuts, cooking until peanuts begin to pop. Add soda, stirring quickly. add vanilla and pour into buttered pan. Cool and cut into squares.

DIVINITY FUDGE

1 can corn syrup
3 cups sugar
1 cup water

3 egg whites
½ cup chopped nuts

Cook the syrup, sugar and water until a soft ball forms, when tested in cold water. Pour gradually over stiffly beaten egg whites. Beat until cold, add nuts. Pour into a buttered dish and cut in squares when it hardens.

LENA'S MOLASSES PULLED CANDY

6 tablespoons molasses
7 tablespoons water
4 tablespoons sugar

¼ pound butter
½ teaspoon vanilla

Boil molasses, water, butter and sugar briskly until it brittles when tested in water. Add vanilla. Pour in dripping pan. When cool enough to handle, pull until very stiff and cut in pieces.

PRALINES

2 cups white sugar
1 cup Old-Fashioned brown sugar
2 cups cold water

1 teaspoon vanilla
2 tablespoons butter
Pecan halves

Cook two minutes or until threads form. Add butter. Add pecans. Then drop in spoonfulls on wet board or platter or buttered tray or waxed paper.

SUGARED NUTS

1 cup white sugar
¼ cup brown sugar
⅓ cup water

2 cups nuts
¼ teaspoon vanilla

Boil the sugar and water without stirring until it spins a long thin thread. Remove from stove, add the flavoring and nuts and stir until the nuts are sugar coated.

SALTED NUTS

1 pound nuts
2 rolling teaspoons butter

1 tablespoon salt

Put nuts into a shallow pan and add the butter, then sprinkle with salt. Put into oven and let brown. Stir the nuts as you bake so that salt and butter can be blended. Let it remain in oven for 15 minutes.

ICE CREAMS AND SHERBETS

LENA'S WATERMELON ICE CREAM

1½ pints whipping cream
½ cup raisins
   Green coloring
½ cup sugar

5 cups or 1¼ quarts strawberry sherbet or other sherbet of reddish color

Whip cream until stiff, add sugar, and color one-half green. Line inside of mold with layer of the green cream to simulate the watermelon rind. Put in a layer of white cream next to the green. In center put layer of 3 cups of sherbet, sprinkling this with raisins. Fill mold with remaining two cups sherbet. Place wax paper over all. Put cover on mold, pack in equal parts ice and salt, let stand for four hours.

To serve: Remove mold from ice and wipe thoroughly to get rid of all salt. Take off top of mold and invert mold on a large platter. Cover mold with a hot towel until the cream leaves the sides of the mold.

OLD-FASHIONED CUSTARD ICE CREAM

1 quart milk
6 eggs
1 pint cream

1½ cups sugar
1 vanilla bean

Beat eggs until light, and add sugar. Heat milk to boiling point, add egg and sugar mixture. Cook until slightly thickened. Remove from fire and let cool. Whip the cream and then add to the first mixture. Split vanilla bean, scrape inside and then add bean and scrapings. Freeze with equal parts of ice and salt. When frozen, remove dasher and pack. Set aside until ready to serve.

EGG NOG ICE CREAM

2 quarts milk
1 pint whipping cream
6 eggs

2½ cups sugar
½ cup Bourbon whiskey

Beat eggs until light, add sugar, beat a few minutes longer. Heat milk to a boiling point, add first mixture to the milk, let cook 10 minutes. Remove from fire; when cool, add stiffly beaten cream and whiskey. Freeze with equal parts of salt and ice.

PEACH MOUSSE

1 No. 2 size can peaches
4 oranges
3 lemons
½ cup Confectioner's sugar

1 cup sugar
½ cup chopped nuts
1 pint whipping cream
1 teaspoon vanilla

Squeeze oranges and lemons. Mash the peaches through colander, using juice and all. Add to the peach mixture lemon and orange juices and granulated sugar. Whip the cream, when partly stiff add confectioner's sugar, nuts and vanilla. Continue to whip until firm. Pour the first mixture into an air-tight mold then pour over this the cream mixture. Line the top with wax paper then place cover on mold. Pack in equal parts of ice and salt for 4 hours or more. When ready to serve reverse on a platter and garnish with whipped cream if desired.

BAKED ALASKA

1 quart vanilla ice cream
1 medium size Angel Food cake
4 egg whites
6 tablespoons confectioner's sugar

½ teaspoon vanilla
1 teaspoon cream of tartar

Scoop out the center of the cake, forming a shell thick enough to hold the ice cream firmly. Beat egg white until it begins to foam, add cream of tartar and beat until stiff and dry. Add sugar, one spoon at a time until it has all been added. Continue to beat. Add vanilla. Fill the cavity of the cake with ice cream. Ice the cake thinly around with the egg white and pile the balance of it on top. Put under a slow flame or in the upper part of a very hot oven to brown quickly. Serve immediately.

ANGEL PARFAIT

⅔ cup sugar
⅔ cup water
2 egg whites

1½ cups heavy whipped cream
1 teaspoon almond flavoring *or*
2 teaspoons vanilla flavoring

Mix the sugar and water and boil until a long thread spins from the end of a spoon. Pour slowly on the stiffly beaten egg whites. Beat until smooth. When cool fold in the whipped cream and flavoring. Pour into a mold, line top of mold with wax paper then place cover on mold and pack in a mixture of two parts of finely chopped ice to one part of coarse salt. Let remain for five hours. Serve in tall glasses with crushed fruit. Top with whipped cream and a cherry.

Because of the richness of the mixture, it does not need to be stirred while freezing.

In packing it the ice and salt must cover the mold which has been sealed tightly to keep the salt out. Pack this dessert in a pail or bucket with holes to allow water to drain while freezing.

FRESH STRAWBERRY SHERBET

4 cups strawberries
3 cups water

3 cups sugar
Juice of 3 lemons

Wash and press strawberries through a sieve until the pulp is dried. Add sugar, water, lemon juice. Freeze in equal parts of ice and salt.

ORANGE SHERBET

4 cups orange juice
3 cups sugar

3 cups water
Juice of 3 lemons

Mix in order given and freeze in equal parts of ice and salt. Sherbet can be served very attractively in orange baskets. Baskets are made by placing an orange with the stem up then cutting on both sides of the stem, half way down, then across on both sides. Scoop out inside pulp and scallop edges of basket. Place on plate and surround with orange leaves.

PINEAPPLE SHERBET

2 cups crushed canned pineapple   4 lemons
or   3 cups sugar
2 cups grated fresh pineapple   1½ quarts water

Squeeze lemons and strain. Mix in order given. Freeze with equal parts of ice and salt.

WATERMELON SHERBET

Cut 1 ripe melon in half, scoop out inside pulp and squeeze until dry. Strain the juice. To every pint of juice, use one cup sugar, one cup water, ½ lemon. Freeze with equal parts of ice and salt. A very attractive way to serve the sherbet is to scallop the rind and place sherbet back into it and serve.

FRESH PEACH SHERBET

4 cups peaches   3 cups sugar
3 cups water   Juice of 3 lemons

Peel and crush peaches. Add sugar, water, lemon juice. Freeze in equal parts of ice and salt. Serve in sherbet glasses topped with sliced peaches.

FROZEN MARSHMALLOW TORTONI

1 pint whipping cream   ¼ pound marshmallows
2 tablespoons sherry   ¼ pound crystallized cherries
½ cup powdered sugar   ¼ pound shelled walnuts

Break marshmallows into small pieces. Dip fingers in cold water to prevent marshmallows from sticking to fingers while preparing. Chop cherries and walnuts fine.

Whip cream and add sugar, just before cream becomes stiff. Fold in marshmallows, cherries, walnuts and sherry. Pour in mold, cover with wax paper and place cover of mold on tight. Pack in equal parts ice and salt and let remain for four hours or more. Be careful to wipe off all salt and water when taking out. Cover with hot, moist cloth and reverse on platter. Serve on platter decorated with whipped cream.

BEVERAGES

CHAMPAGNE PUNCH

1 teaspoon simple sugar syrup	1½ wine glass maraschino juice
3 slices of orange	1½ wine glass white curacoa
3 slices of lemon	1 wine glass of sherry
1 rind of lemon	1 quart champagne
1 slice cucumber peel	1 quart soda water
1 teaspoon Pechaud bitters	
1½ wine glass or 2 ounces of brandy	

For mixing use a large container. Mix ingredients as listed. Pour into a bowl over a good quantity of crushed ice. Serve in champagne glasses and ornament with fresh mint or sliced fruit. This will serve 24 people.

LENA'S OLD FASHIONED LEMONADE

1 cup sugar	1 pint water
⅓ cup lemon juice	

Make syrup by boiling sugar and water 12 minutes. Add fruit juice, cool and dilute with iced water to suit individual taste. Lemon syrup may be bottled and kept on hand to use as needed.

BRANDY OR WHISKEY PUNCH

1 quart brandy or whiskey	1¼ cups powdered sugar
1 quart charged water	½ pint curacoa
Juice 7 lemons	½ jigger Grenadine Syrup
Juice 2 oranges	

Dissolve sugar in as small an amount of warm water as possible. Then add ingredients as follows: grenadine, lemon juice, orange juice, curacoa, whiskey or brandy. Place large block of ice in punch bowl, pour in mixture and add charged water.

FRUIT PUNCH

2 cups chopped or crushed pineapple
Juice 6 lemons
Juice 6 oranges

1 pint tea
2 quarts of gingerale *or* charged water
2 cups sugar

Boil water and sugar 10 minutes. When cool add rest of ingredients and let cool one hour, or more. Add charged water or ginger ale. Serve with crushed ice or sherbet.

EGG NOG—Cold

1 pint milk
1 pint whipping cream
6 egg yolks

1 cup sugar
1 cup whiskey
2 teaspoons nutmeg

Beat egg yolks until light and lemon colored. Add sugar and continue to beat until thoroughly combined. Add the whiskey and one teaspoon nutmeg to the mixture. Add milk stirring well. Fold in stiffly beaten whipping cream. Sprinkle the top with the remaining nutmeg and serve.

EGG NOG—Hot

1 pint milk
1 pint whipping cream
6 egg yolks

4 egg whites
1 cup sugar
2 teaspoons nutmeg

Separate eggs, beat yolks until light. Add sugar and one teaspoon nutmeg, beat again. Heat milk and cream to boiling point. Add to sugar and egg mixture, cook 3 minutes. Whip egg whites until stiff, fold in while Egg Nog is still hot. Place a silver spoon in each glass and fill ¾ full of Egg Nog. Sprinkle a little of the remaining nutmeg in each glass. Flavor with whiskey to suit your taste.

COCOA

2 teaspoons sugar	1 cup milk
2 teaspoons cocoa	¼ teaspoon vanilla

Mix sugar and cocoa and boil with two tablespoons of water for 2 minutes. Add milk and just bring to the boiling point. Add vanilla and serve.

CREOLE DRIPPED COFFEE

Put 5 tablespoons of coffee with chicory or 7 tablespoons of coffee without chicory in a coffee pot. Pour 3 tablespoons of luke warm water over the coffee to allow it to swell. Continue to drip with boiling hot water until 5 cupsful are made. This is extra strong coffee with chicory.

In case a lighter coffee is desired, one more cup of hot water may be added. It is a custom to serve Creole coffee plain black, or with milk.

CAFE AU LAIT

Café au lait is made by adding ½ cup of cream and ½ cup of milk to ¼ cup of strong coffee. Let it come to a boil and serve.

SELECTED MENUS FOR BREAKFAST

For a Light Breakfast:
 Fruit Juice or Fruit
 Cereal
 Buttered or Dry Toast
 Tea, Coffee or Milk

Heavier Breakfast:
 I Fruit Juice or Fruit
 Cereal
 Poached Egg on Toast
 2 Slices of Melba Toast
 Tea, Coffee or Milk

 II Fruit Juice or Fruit
 2 Fried Eggs
 Graham Muffins
 Butter
 Tea, Coffee or Milk

 III Fruit Juice or Fruit
 Cream Cheese
 Hot Buttered Biscuits
 2 Slices Bacon
 Tea, Coffee or Milk

 IV Fruit Juice or Fruit
 Country Pork Sausage
 Waffles and Cane Syrup
 Tea, Coffee or Milk

SELECTED MENUS FOR FORMAL AND INFORMAL LUNCHEONS AND DINNERS

I Course
Clear Bouillon
Curly Toast

II Course
Stuffed Broilers
Spinach Souffle
Pineapple Fritters
Hot Buttered Rolls

III Course
Salad: Artichoke Mousse
Mayonnaise Dressing
Saltine or Buttered Crackers

IV Course
Dessert: Lena's Watermelon Ice Cream
Café Noir

1 Course
Shrimp Cocktail
Buttered Wafers

II Course
Filet Mignon
Fresh Mushroom Sauce

Potato Puffs
Shoe-string Carrots and String Beans
Hot Buttered Rolls

III Course
Salad: Roquefort Cheese Dressing on head lettuce
Saltine Crackers

IV Course
Dessert: Egg Nog Ice Cream served in Meringue Shell
Café Noir

—◆❀◆—

I Course
Turtle Soup
Melba Toast

II Course
Breast of Turkey with Sweetbreads and Ham Sauce
Boiled Cauliflower with Drawn Butter Sauce
Scalloped Sweet Potatoes and Pineapple
Hot Buttered Biscuits
Green Salad served with the dinner

III Course
Dessert: Peach Sherbet
Café Noir

—◆❀◆—

I Course
Avocado Cocktail
Buttered or Saltine Crackers

II Course
Broiled Steak
Hashed Brown Potatoes
Fried Onion Rings
Petit Pois
Candied Carrots

III Course
Dessert: Strawberry Shortcake
Café Noir

—◦◦⊰⊱◦◦—

I Course
Cherry and Cantaloupe Cocktail

II Course
Fried Chicken
Corn Fritters
Creamed Turnips
Chilled Sliced Tomatoes with Lettuce and French Dressing
Corn Sticks

III Course
Dessert: Date and Nut Pudding
Café Noir

—◦◦⊰⊱◦◦—

I Course
Hearts of Artichokes with Fluffy Egg Dressing on
Shredded Lettuce
Cheese Rolls

II Course
Seafood and Asparagus Vol-au-vent
Baked Mirletons
Jellied Cucumber and Pineapple Salad

III Course
Dessert: Baked Prune Whip
Café Noir

MENUS FOR PLAIN LUNCHEONS

Oyster en Brochette
Fried Grits
Green Salad with French Dressing
French Bread and Butter
Dessert: Fresh Fruit

Chicken Croquette or
Crab Cutlets with Lena's Red Sauce
Shoe String Potatoes
Vegetable Salad
Hot Biscuits with Butter
Dessert: Baked Apples and Cream

Pineapple and Cucumber Salad
Cream Dressing
Curly Toast
Spanish Omelet
Spoon Bread
Dessert: Chocolate Ice Box Cake

Seafood or Fruit Cocktail
Lena's Lamb Chops and Pineapple
Spinach Souffle
Potato Puffs
Dessert: Hot Gingerbread with Hard Sauce

If drinks are served at luncheon
For Winter: Black Coffee or Hot Tea
For Summer: Iced Coffee or Iced Tea
When wine is served:
White Wine with fish
Red Wine with meats
Olives and celery are very appetizing served with the first course.

COLD AND HOT SUPPER DISHES

COLD

Baked Ham with Pastry or with Brown Sugar and Spice
Daube Glace
Cold cuts consisting of Turkey, Tongue, Lamb and Sausages
Stuffed Eggs
Potato Salad
Green Salad
Chicken Salad
Stuffed Whole Tomato with Crab or Shrimp Salad
Stuffed Celery
Apple and Orange Compote

HOT

Creamed Sweetbreads and Mushrooms or
Creamed Chicken, Shrimp, Crab and Oyster served either on
toast, pastry shell, patties, timbales or in a vol-au-vent.
Welsh Rarebit
Nuts and Mints

USES FOR LEFT OVERS

Turkey or chicken may be used as Turkey or Chicken Filet with Spaghetti. The carcass may be used as stock for soups or gumbo.

Meats that have been boiled for soups or bouillon may be made into croquettes and served with a sauce.

Ham bones may be used for flavoring cabbage or red beans.

Left over vegetables such as snap beans, carrots, cauliflower, turnips can be used with cream sauce. Cauliflower may be made into balls. Left over potatoes can be made into potato cakes.

Left over rice can be made into rice pudding or rice dressing.

Stale cakes can be used with hot sauces.

MISCELLANEOUS INFORMATION

CARAMEL COLORING

½ cup sugar   1 cup water

Put sugar in frying pan and cook until it is dark brown. Add water and boil until all the sugar has melted. Let cool, strain and put in a jar. This caramel may be used for coloring soups, meats and for icings.

METHOD FOR MAKING AN EGG WASH

2 eggs   ¼ teaspoon cayenne
½ cup milk   1 tablespoon salt
½ teaspoon white pepper

Beat whole eggs until light, add milk and seasonings. This amount can be used for one 2 pound fried chicken, 2 veal rounds or 6 chops.

GENERAL DIRECTION FOR COOKING CAULIFLOWER

Remove the leaves from the cauliflower. Cut off the stalk and soak for thirty minutes with the head down in enough cold water to cover the whole cauliflower. Cook for twenty minutes or until soft, in boiling water into which the lemon juice has been squeezed. Drain and separate the flowerets, or serve whole.

MAKING OF ROUX

Heat fat then add flour, stir until light brown add onions and continue to stir until onions and flour are a golden brown.

GENERAL RULES IN PREPARATION AND REMOVAL OF JELLIED SALADS AND DESSERTS

1. Soak gelatine in cold water 5 minutes.
2. Dissolve in hot liquid according to recipe.
3. Never fail to moisten mold with cold water before pouring in mixture to be jelled—this helps in removal.
4. Wrap hot towel around mold for a few seconds until the salad is loosened in the mold. Then place platter on top of mold and invert.

GENERAL DIRECTIONS FOR PACKING MOLDS

In packing any mold it must be packed in a container with holes to allow the water to drip out while freezing

It should be packed in equal parts of ice and salt.

The mold must remain in ice for 4 hours or more. Remove the mold, and let cold water run over it. Wipe dry with a cloth and remove cover. Insert knife around edges of mold and place a platter over mold and reverse.

ROLL SECTION

In making rolls the liquid measure is always exact but owing to variation in the size of the egg, the amount of flour to be used can never be exactly determined. So in describing the amount of flour necessary, we use the term "rolling consistency" which means adding a sufficient amount of flour to other ingredients until the consistency of the dough is such that it will not stick to the hands, the board or the rolling pin.

HOMEMADE VOL-AU-VENT
(Use Plain Pastry Recipe)

Turn deep oblong or round pan upside down on table. Grease entire outer sides and bottom of pan and mold pastry dough over this. Prick dough with fork to prevent bubbling and trim edges with knife. Place in oven and bake in 300° oven for 25 minutes until dry and delicately browned.

DIRECTIONS FOR BAKING HOT BREADS AND CAKES

Always put either bread or cake into lower half of top oven until dough has risen to its full size—then place in top part of same oven to brown.

STANDARD METHOD OF MIXING A CAKE

Cream butter, and add sugar gradually. Separate eggs, and add yolks to butter and sugar and mix well. Mix flour and baking powder, sift at least three times and add alternately with the milk to the butter, egg and sugar mixture. Add flavoring. Beat briskly two minutes. Fold in whites of eggs, beaten stiff, but not dry.

USE OF CAKE TINS

To prepare baking tins:
Grease with unsalted fat. Sift flour into greased tins, then shake out surplus. Fill tin about 2/3 full of batter. Push batter to sides so that cake will rise more evenly. Remove cake from tin while it is still warm. Allow cake to cool on rack before frosting.

BAKING OF A CAKE

Time is divided into four quarters.
1st quarter—Cake rises and bubbles.
2nd quarter—Rises and browns.
3rd quarter—Brown all over—continues to rise.
4th quarter—Finishes baking, shrinks from sides, rebounds when touched with the finger (gently).

HOW TO MEASURE INGREDIENTS

Correct measurements and definite proportions are absolutely necessary to insure successful results. Measuring cups holding one-half pint are marked on the sides in thirds and fourths. These are the standard measuring cups used whenever scientific cookery is taught. Two of these cups will be found very convenient. Use one for measuring dry ingredients, and the other for measuring fats used for shortening and liquids. Flour and meal should always be sifted before measuring.

To Fill A Cup. A cupful means all the cup will hold. Toss dry ingredients into a cup with a tablespoon until the ingredients reach the line on the measuring cup denoting a full cup.

Tablespoons of regulation size are filled, and then leveled with a knife; teaspoons are filled the same. When dividing either teaspoon or tablespoon, fill spoon, level with knife, then place the end of knife blade toward handle of spoon, dividing lengthwise of bowl of spoon, leaving spoon half full. Dividing the half crosswise leaves one-fourth. Dividing the fourth crosswise leaves one-eighth. Less than one-eighth is called a few grains.

Rolling spoon is a heaping spoon full level on each side with a knife.

Measuring Fats. Fats used for shortening are packed solidly in cups, tablespoons and teaspoons, and leveled with a knife. Place the cup to be filled on a saucer and fill to cup mark. Tablespoon and teaspoonfull mean all these spoons will hold of liquids.

Combining Ingredients. There are four motions used in combining ingredients. Stirring, beating, cutting and folding. Stirring is combining ingredients by circular motion, enlarging and repeating these motions until all ingredients are thoroughly blended.

OVEN TEMPERATURES

	Degrees F.
Very hot	450 to 500
Hot	400 to 450
Moderately hot	375 to 400
Moderate	325 to 375
Very hot moderate	300 to 325
Slow	250 to 300
Very slow	225 to 250

ABBREVIATIONS

Tsp.—teaspoon   Tbsp.—tablespoon
F. G.—Few grains

DRY MEASURE

2 pints—1 quart   4 pecks—1 bushel
8 quarts—1 peck   4 bushels—1 barrel

LIQUID MEASURES

4 fluid ounces—1 gill   4 quarts—1 gallon
4 gills—1 pint $31\frac{1}{2}$ gallons—1 barrel
2 pints—1 quart   2 barrels—1 hogshead

VARIOUS WEIGHTS

2 cups liquid—1 pound
2 cups shortening—1 pound
4 cups flour—1 pound
$1\frac{7}{8}$ cups rice—1 pound
2 cups chopped meat—1 pound
1 square chocolate—1 ounce
4 tablespoons grated chocolate—1 ounce
4 tablespoons cocoa—1 ounce
1 cup granulated sugar—$\frac{1}{2}$ pound
1 cup butter—$\frac{1}{2}$ pound
1 cup lard—$\frac{1}{2}$ pound
1 cup flour—$\frac{1}{4}$ pound
1 cup rice—$\frac{1}{2}$ pound
1 cup corn meal—5 ounces
1 cup stale bread crumbs—2 ounces

INDEX

Candy
  divinity fudge, 119
  molasses pulled, 119
  peanut, 119
  pralines, 120
Carrots
  à la king, 80
  candied, 74
  shoe-string, 76
Cauliflower
  balls, 78
  directions for cooking, 135
  panees, 77
Celery, stuffed, 54
Charlotte russe, 98
Cheese
  appetizers, 1–2
  balls, 3
Chicken
  à la king, 60
  aspic, 46
  broiled, 64–65
  broilers, baked, 59
  broilers, stuffed, 67
  country fried, 57
  Creole fried, 57
  croquette, 68
  Maryland, 61
  mousse, 49–50
  salad, 42
  salad sandwich, 117–118
Cocktails
  avocado, 6
  cherry and cantaloupe, 5
  fruit, 5
  seafood, 6
  watermelon, 6
Cocoa, 127
Codfish balls, 12
Coffee, Creole dripped, 127
Coloring, caramel, 135
Compote
  cherry apples, 73
  orange, 73
  pear, 73–74
Cookies
  ice box, 106
  oatmeal, 107
  sliced nut, 107
  sugar, 106

Corn
  boiled, green, 81
  clear soup, 20
  pudding, 81–82
  soup, cream of, 21
Crab
  aspic, 47
  cutlets, 15
  fricasse, 11
  mousse, 9
  omelet, 39
  salad, 43
  soup, cream of, 21
  stuffed or deviled, 13
Cream puffs, 109
Custard, baked, 90

Date
  bar, 108
  and nut cake, 102
  and nut pudding, 89
  tart, 108
Daube
  glace, 58
  with gravy, 58
Doughnuts, 107–108
Duck, wild, roast, 61

Eggs
  creamed, 37
  fried, 35
  poached, 35
  scalloped, 36
  scalloped with tomatoes, 37
  scrambled, 35
  stuffed, 37
Egg nog, 126
Egg wash, 135
Eggplant, fried, 82

Fats, measuring, 138
Filet mignon, 67
Filling
  cream, 94
  See also pie filling
Fish
  broiled, 13
  fried tenderloined, 15
  scaled, 8
  vol-au-vent, 12–13

A CATALOG OF SELECTED
DOVER BOOKS
IN ALL FIELDS OF INTEREST

A CATALOG OF SELECTED DOVER
BOOKS IN ALL FIELDS OF INTEREST

DRAWINGS OF REMBRANDT, edited by Seymour Slive. Updated Lippmann, Hofstede de Groot edition, with definitive scholarly apparatus. All portraits, biblical sketches, landscapes, nudes. Oriental figures, classical studies, together with selection of work by followers. 550 illustrations. Total of 630pp. 9⅛ × 12¼.
21485-0, 21486-9 Pa., Two-vol. set $29.90

GHOST AND HORROR STORIES OF AMBROSE BIERCE, Ambrose Bierce. 24 tales vividly imagined, strangely prophetic, and decades ahead of their time in technical skill: "The Damned Thing," "An Inhabitant of Carcosa," "The Eyes of the Panther," "Moxon's Master," and 20 more. 199pp. 5⅜ × 8½. 20767-6 Pa. $4.95

ETHICAL WRITINGS OF MAIMONIDES, Maimonides. Most significant ethical works of great medieval sage, newly translated for utmost precision, readability. Laws Concerning Character Traits, Eight Chapters, more. 192pp. 5⅜ × 8½.
24522-5 Pa. $4.50

THE EXPLORATION OF THE COLORADO RIVER AND ITS CANYONS, J. W. Powell. Full text of Powell's 1,000-mile expedition down the fabled Colorado in 1869. Superb account of terrain, geology, vegetation, Indians, famine, mutiny, treacherous rapids, mighty canyons, during exploration of last unknown part of continental U.S. 400pp. 5⅜ × 8½. 20094-9 Pa. $7.95

HISTORY OF PHILOSOPHY, Julián Marías. Clearest one-volume history on the market. Every major philosopher and dozens of others, to Existentialism and later. 505pp. 5⅜ × 8½. 21739-6 Pa. $9.95

ALL ABOUT LIGHTNING, Martin A. Uman. Highly readable non-technical survey of nature and causes of lightning, thunderstorms, ball lightning, St. Elmo's Fire, much more. Illustrated. 192pp. 5⅜ × 8½. 25237-X Pa. $5.95

SAILING ALONE AROUND THE WORLD, Captain Joshua Slocum. First man to sail around the world, alone, in small boat. One of great feats of seamanship told in delightful manner. 67 illustrations. 294pp. 5⅜ × 8½. 20326-3 Pa. $4.95

LETTERS AND NOTES ON THE MANNERS, CUSTOMS AND CONDITIONS OF THE NORTH AMERICAN INDIANS, George Catlin. Classic account of life among Plains Indians: ceremonies, hunt, warfare, etc. 312 plates. 572pp. of text. 6⅛ × 9¼. 22118-0, 22119-9, Pa. Two-vol. set $17.90

ALASKA: The Harriman Expedition, 1899, John Burroughs, John Muir, et al. Informative, engrossing accounts of two-month, 9,000-mile expedition. Native peoples, wildlife, forests, geography, salmon industry, glaciers, more. Profusely illustrated. 240 black-and-white line drawings. 124 black-and-white photographs. 3 maps. Index. 576pp. 5⅜ × 8½. 25109-8 Pa. $11.95

THE BOOK OF BEASTS: Being a Translation from a Latin Bestiary of the Twelfth Century, T. H. White. Wonderful catalog real and fanciful beasts: manticore, griffin, phoenix, amphivius, jaculus, many more. White's witty erudite commentary on scientific, historical aspects. Fascinating glimpse of medieval mind. Illustrated. 296pp. 5⅜ × 8¼. (Available in U.S. only) 24609-4 Pa. $6.95

FRANK LLOYD WRIGHT: ARCHITECTURE AND NATURE With 160 Illustrations, Donald Hoffmann. Profusely illustrated study of influence of nature—especially prairie—on Wright's designs for Fallingwater, Robie House, Guggenheim Museum, other masterpieces. 96pp. 9¼ × 10¾. 25098-9 Pa. $8.95

FRANK LLOYD WRIGHT'S FALLINGWATER, Donald Hoffmann. Wright's famous waterfall house: planning and construction of organic idea. History of site, owners, Wright's personal involvement. Photographs of various stages of building. Preface by Edgar Kaufmann, Jr. 100 illustrations. 112pp. 9¼ × 10.
23671-4 Pa. $8.95

YEARS WITH FRANK LLOYD WRIGHT: Apprentice to Genius, Edgar Tafel. Insightful memoir by a former apprentice presents a revealing portrait of Wright the man, the inspired teacher, the greatest American architect. 372 black-and-white illustrations. Preface. Index. vi + 228pp. 8¼ × 11. 24801-1 Pa. $10.95

THE STORY OF KING ARTHUR AND HIS KNIGHTS, Howard Pyle. Enchanting version of King Arthur fable has delighted generations with imaginative narratives of exciting adventures and unforgettable illustrations by the author. 41 illustrations. xviii + 313pp. 6⅛ × 9¼. 21445-1 Pa. $6.95

THE GODS OF THE EGYPTIANS, E. A. Wallis Budge. Thorough coverage of numerous gods of ancient Egypt by foremost Egyptologist. Information on evolution of cults, rites and gods; the cult of Osiris; the Book of the Dead and its rites; the sacred animals and birds; Heaven and Hell; and more. 956pp. 6⅛ × 9¼.
22055-9, 22056-7 Pa., Two-vol. set $21.90

A THEOLOGICO-POLITICAL TREATISE, Benedict Spinoza. Also contains unfinished *Political Treatise*. Great classic on religious liberty, theory of government on common consent. R. Elwes translation. Total of 421pp. 5⅜ × 8½.
20249-6 Pa. $7.95

INCIDENTS OF TRAVEL IN CENTRAL AMERICA, CHIAPAS, AND YUCATAN, John L. Stephens. Almost single-handed discovery of Maya culture; exploration of ruined cities, monuments, temples; customs of Indians. 115 drawings. 892pp. 5⅜ × 8½. 22404-X, 22405-8 Pa., Two-vol. set $15.90

LOS CAPRICHOS, Francisco Goya. 80 plates of wild, grotesque monsters and caricatures. Prado manuscript included. 183pp. 6⅝ × 9⅜. 22384-1 Pa. $5.95

AUTOBIOGRAPHY: The Story of My Experiments with Truth, Mohandas K. Gandhi. Not hagiography, but Gandhi in his own words. Boyhood, legal studies, purification, the growth of the Satyagraha (nonviolent protest) movement. Critical, inspiring work of the man who freed India. 480pp. 5⅜ × 8½. (Available in U.S. only)
24593-4 Pa. $6.95

ILLUSTRATED DICTIONARY OF HISTORIC ARCHITECTURE, edited by Cyril M. Harris. Extraordinary compendium of clear, concise definitions for over 5,000 important architectural terms complemented by over 2,000 line drawings. Covers full spectrum of architecture from ancient ruins to 20th-century Modernism. Preface. 592pp. 7½ × 9⅝. 24444-X Pa. $15.95

THE NIGHT BEFORE CHRISTMAS, Clement Moore. Full text, and woodcuts from original 1848 book. Also critical, historical material. 19 illustrations. 40pp. 4⅝ × 6. 22797-9 Pa. $2.50

THE LESSON OF JAPANESE ARCHITECTURE: 165 Photographs, Jiro Harada. Memorable gallery of 165 photographs taken in the 1930's of exquisite Japanese homes of the well-to-do and historic buildings. 13 line diagrams. 192pp. 8⅝ × 11¼. 24778-3 Pa. $10.95

THE AUTOBIOGRAPHY OF CHARLES DARWIN AND SELECTED LETTERS, edited by Francis Darwin. The fascinating life of eccentric genius composed of an intimate memoir by Darwin (intended for his children); commentary by his son, Francis; hundreds of fragments from notebooks, journals, papers; and letters to and from Lyell, Hooker, Huxley, Wallace and Henslow. xi + 365pp. 5⅜ × 8. 20479-0 Pa. $6.95

WONDERS OF THE SKY: Observing Rainbows, Comets, Eclipses, the Stars and Other Phenomena, Fred Schaaf. Charming, easy-to-read poetic guide to all manner of celestial events visible to the naked eye. Mock suns, glories, Belt of Venus, more. Illustrated. 299pp. 5¼ × 8¼. 24402-4 Pa. $7.95

BURNHAM'S CELESTIAL HANDBOOK, Robert Burnham, Jr. Thorough guide to the stars beyond our solar system. Exhaustive treatment. Alphabetical by constellation: Andromeda to Cetus in Vol. 1; Chamaeleon to Orion in Vol. 2; and Pavo to Vulpecula in Vol. 3. Hundreds of illustrations. Index in Vol. 3. 2,000pp. 6⅛ × 9¼. 23567-X, 23568-8, 23673-0 Pa., Three-vol. set $41.85

STAR NAMES: Their Lore and Meaning, Richard Hinckley Allen. Fascinating history of names various cultures have given to constellations and literary and folkloristic uses that have been made of stars. Indexes to subjects. Arabic and Greek names. Biblical references. Bibliography. 563pp. 5⅜ × 8½. 21079-0 Pa. $8.95

THIRTY YEARS THAT SHOOK PHYSICS: The Story of Quantum Theory, George Gamow. Lucid, accessible introduction to influential theory of energy and matter. Careful explanations of Dirac's anti-particles, Bohr's model of the atom, much more. 12 plates. Numerous drawings. 240pp. 5⅜ × 8½. 24895-X Pa. $5.95

CHINESE DOMESTIC FURNITURE IN PHOTOGRAPHS AND MEASURED DRAWINGS, Gustav Ecke. A rare volume, now affordably priced for antique collectors, furniture buffs and art historians. Detailed review of styles ranging from early Shang to late Ming. Unabridged republication. 161 black-and-white drawings, photos. Total of 224pp. 8⅜ × 11¼. (Available in U.S. only) 25171-3 Pa. $13.95

VINCENT VAN GOGH: A Biography, Julius Meier-Graefe. Dynamic, penetrating study of artist's life, relationship with brother, Theo, painting techniques, travels, more. Readable, engrossing. 160pp. 5⅜ × 8½. (Available in U.S. only) 25253-1 Pa. $4.95

HOW TO WRITE, Gertrude Stein. Gertrude Stein claimed anyone could understand her unconventional writing—here are clues to help. Fascinating improvisations, language experiments, explanations illuminate Stein's craft and the art of writing. Total of 414pp. 4⅝ × 6⅜. 23144-5 Pa. $6.95

ADVENTURES AT SEA IN THE GREAT AGE OF SAIL: Five Firsthand Narratives, edited by Elliot Snow. Rare true accounts of exploration, whaling, shipwreck, fierce natives, trade, shipboard life, more. 33 illustrations. Introduction. 353pp. 5⅜ × 8½. 25177-2 Pa. $8.95

THE HERBAL OR GENERAL HISTORY OF PLANTS, John Gerard. Classic descriptions of about 2,850 plants—with over 2,700 illustrations—includes Latin and English names, physical descriptions, varieties, time and place of growth, more. 2,706 illustrations. xlv + 1,678pp. 8½ × 12¼. 23147-X Cloth. $75.00

DOROTHY AND THE WIZARD IN OZ, L. Frank Baum. Dorothy and the Wizard visit the center of the Earth, where people are vegetables, glass houses grow and Oz characters reappear. Classic sequel to *Wizard of Oz.* 256pp. 5⅜ × 8.
24714-7 Pa. $5.95

SONGS OF EXPERIENCE: Facsimile Reproduction with 26 Plates in Full Color, William Blake. This facsimile of Blake's original "Illuminated Book" reproduces 26 full-color plates from a rare 1826 edition. Includes "The Tyger," "London," "Holy Thursday," and other immortal poems. 26 color plates. Printed text of poems. 48pp. 5¼ × 7. 24636-1 Pa. $3.95

SONGS OF INNOCENCE, William Blake. The first and most popular of Blake's famous "Illuminated Books," in a facsimile edition reproducing all 31 brightly colored plates. Additional printed text of each poem. 64pp. 5¼ × 7.
22764-2 Pa. $3.95

PRECIOUS STONES, Max Bauer. Classic, thorough study of diamonds, rubies, emeralds, garnets, etc.: physical character, occurrence, properties, use, similar topics. 20 plates, 8 in color. 94 figures. 659pp. 6⅛ × 9¼.
21910-0, 21911-9 Pa., Two-vol. set $15.90

ENCYCLOPEDIA OF VICTORIAN NEEDLEWORK, S. F. A. Caulfeild and Blanche Saward. Full, precise descriptions of stitches, techniques for dozens of needlecrafts—most exhaustive reference of its kind. Over 800 figures. Total of 679pp. 8⅜ × 11. Two volumes. Vol. 1 22800-2 Pa. $11.95
Vol. 2 22801-0 Pa. $11.95

THE MARVELOUS LAND OF OZ, L. Frank Baum. Second Oz book, the Scarecrow and Tin Woodman are back with hero named Tip, Oz magic. 136 illustrations. 287pp. 5⅜ × 8½. 20692-0 Pa. $5.95

WILD FOWL DECOYS, Joel Barber. Basic book on the subject, by foremost authority and collector. Reveals history of decoy making and rigging, place in American culture, different kinds of decoys, how to make them, and how to use them. 140 plates. 156pp. 7⅞ × 10¾. 20011-6 Pa. $8.95

HISTORY OF LACE, Mrs. Bury Palliser. Definitive, profusely illustrated chronicle of lace from earliest times to late 19th century. Laces of Italy, Greece, England, France, Belgium, etc. Landmark of needlework scholarship. 266 illustrations. 672pp. 6⅛ × 9¼. 24742-2 Pa. $14.95

ILLUSTRATED GUIDE TO SHAKER FURNITURE, Robert Meader. All furniture and appurtenances, with much on unknown local styles. 235 photos. 146pp. 9 × 12. 22819-3 Pa. $8.95

WHALE SHIPS AND WHALING: A Pictorial Survey, George Francis Dow. Over 200 vintage engravings, drawings, photographs of barks, brigs, cutters, other vessels. Also harpoons, lances, whaling guns, many other artifacts. Comprehensive text by foremost authority. 207 black-and-white illustrations. 288pp. 6 × 9. 24808-9 Pa. $9.95

THE BERTRAMS, Anthony Trollope. Powerful portrayal of blind self-will and thwarted ambition includes one of Trollope's most heartrending love stories. 497pp. 5⅜ × 8½. 25119-5 Pa. $9.95

ADVENTURES WITH A HAND LENS, Richard Headstrom. Clearly written guide to observing and studying flowers and grasses, fish scales, moth and insect wings, egg cases, buds, feathers, seeds, leaf scars, moss, molds, ferns, common crystals, etc.—all with an ordinary, inexpensive magnifying glass. 209 exact line drawings aid in your discoveries. 220pp. 5⅜ × 8½. 23330-8 Pa. $4.95

RODIN ON ART AND ARTISTS, Auguste Rodin. Great sculptor's candid, wide-ranging comments on meaning of art; great artists; relation of sculpture to poetry, painting, music; philosophy of life, more. 76 superb black-and-white illustrations of Rodin's sculpture, drawings and prints. 119pp. 8⅜ × 11¼. 24487-3 Pa. $7.95

FIFTY CLASSIC FRENCH FILMS, 1912–1982: A Pictorial Record, Anthony Slide. Memorable stills from Grand Illusion, Beauty and the Beast, Hiroshima, Mon Amour, many more. Credits, plot synopses, reviews, etc. 160pp. 8¼ × 11. 25256-6 Pa. $11.95

THE PRINCIPLES OF PSYCHOLOGY, William James. Famous long course complete, unabridged. Stream of thought, time perception, memory, experimental methods; great work decades ahead of its time. 94 figures. 1,391pp. 5⅜ × 8½. 20381-6, 20382-4 Pa., Two-vol. set $23.90

BODIES IN A BOOKSHOP, R. T. Campbell. Challenging mystery of blackmail and murder with ingenious plot and superbly drawn characters. In the best tradition of British suspense fiction. 192pp. 5⅜ × 8½. 24720-1 Pa. $4.95

CALLAS: PORTRAIT OF A PRIMA DONNA, George Jellinek. Renowned commentator on the musical scene chronicles incredible career and life of the most controversial, fascinating, influential operatic personality of our time. 64 black-and-white photographs. 416pp. 5⅜ × 8¼. 25047-4 Pa. $8.95

GEOMETRY, RELATIVITY AND THE FOURTH DIMENSION, Rudolph Rucker. Exposition of fourth dimension, concepts of relativity as Flatland characters continue adventures. Popular, easily followed yet accurate, profound. 141 illustrations. 133pp. 5⅜ × 8½. 23400-2 Pa. $4.95

HOUSEHOLD STORIES BY THE BROTHERS GRIMM, with pictures by Walter Crane. 53 classic stories—Rumpelstiltskin, Rapunzel, Hansel and Gretel, the Fisherman and his Wife, Snow White, Tom Thumb, Sleeping Beauty, Cinderella, and so much more—lavishly illustrated with original 19th century drawings. 114 illustrations. x + 269pp. 5⅜ × 8½. 21080-4 Pa. $4.95

CATALOG OF DOVER BOOKS

SUNDIALS, Albert Waugh. Far and away the best, most thorough coverage of ideas, mathematics concerned, types, construction, adjusting anywhere. Over 100 illustrations. 230pp. 5⅜ × 8½. 22947-5 Pa. $5.95

PICTURE HISTORY OF THE NORMANDIE: With 190 Illustrations, Frank O. Braynard. Full story of legendary French ocean liner: Art Deco interiors, design innovations, furnishings, celebrities, maiden voyage, tragic fire, much more. Extensive text. 144pp. 8⅞ × 11¾. 25257-4 Pa. $10.95

THE FIRST AMERICAN COOKBOOK: A Facsimile of "American Cookery," 1796, Amelia Simmons. Facsimile of the first American-written cookbook published in the United States contains authentic recipes for colonial favorites—pumpkin pudding, winter squash pudding, spruce beer, Indian slapjacks, and more. Introductory Essay and Glossary of colonial cooking terms. 80pp. 5⅜ × 8½. 24710-4 Pa. $3.50

101 PUZZLES IN THOUGHT AND LOGIC, C. R. Wylie, Jr. Solve murders and robberies, find out which fishermen are liars, how a blind man could possibly identify a color—purely by your own reasoning! 107pp. 5⅜ × 8½. 20367-0 Pa. $2.50

ANCIENT EGYPTIAN MYTHS AND LEGENDS, Lewis Spence. Examines animism, totemism, fetishism, creation myths, deities, alchemy, art and magic, other topics. Over 50 illustrations. 432pp. 5⅜ × 8½. 26525-0 Pa. $8.95

ANTHROPOLOGY AND MODERN LIFE, Franz Boas. Great anthropologist's classic treatise on race and culture. Introduction by Ruth Bunzel. Only inexpensive paperback edition. 255pp. 5⅜ × 8½. 25245-0 Pa. $6.95

THE TALE OF PETER RABBIT, Beatrix Potter. The inimitable Peter's terrifying adventure in Mr. McGregor's garden, with all 27 wonderful, full-color Potter illustrations. 55pp. 4¼ × 5½. (Available in U.S. only) 22827-4 Pa. $1.75

THREE PROPHETIC SCIENCE FICTION NOVELS, H. G. Wells. *When the Sleeper Wakes, A Story of the Days to Come* and *The Time Machine* (full version). 335pp. 5⅜ × 8½. (Available in U.S. only) 20605-X Pa. $6.95

APICIUS COOKERY AND DINING IN IMPERIAL ROME, edited and translated by Joseph Dommers Vehling. Oldest known cookbook in existence offers readers a clear picture of what foods Romans ate, how they prepared them, etc. 49 illustrations. 301pp. 6⅛ × 9¼. 23563-7 Pa. $7.95

SHAKESPEARE LEXICON AND QUOTATION DICTIONARY, Alexander Schmidt. Full definitions, locations, shades of meaning of every word in plays and poems. More than 50,000 exact quotations. 1,485pp. 6½ × 9¼. 22726-X, 22727-8 Pa., Two-vol. set $31.90

THE WORLD'S GREAT SPEECHES, edited by Lewis Copeland and Lawrence W. Lamm. Vast collection of 278 speeches from Greeks to 1970. Powerful and effective models; unique look at history. 842pp. 5⅜ × 8½. 20468-5 Pa. $12.95

THE BLUE FAIRY BOOK, Andrew Lang. The first, most famous collection, with many familiar tales: Little Red Riding Hood, Aladdin and the Wonderful Lamp, Puss in Boots, Sleeping Beauty, Hansel and Gretel, Rumpelstiltskin; 37 in all. 138 illustrations. 390pp. 5⅜ × 8½. 21437-0 Pa. $6.95

THE STORY OF THE CHAMPIONS OF THE ROUND TABLE, Howard Pyle. Sir Launcelot, Sir Tristram and Sir Percival in spirited adventures of love and triumph retold in Pyle's inimitable style. 50 drawings, 31 full-page. xviii + 329pp. 6½ × 9¼. 21883-X Pa. $7.95

THE MYTHS OF THE NORTH AMERICAN INDIANS, Lewis Spence. Myths and legends of the Algonquins, Iroquois, Pawnees and Sioux with comprehensive historical and ethnological commentary. 36 illustrations. 5⅜ × 8½. 25967-6 Pa. $8.95

GREAT DINOSAUR HUNTERS AND THEIR DISCOVERIES, Edwin H. Colbert. Fascinating, lavishly illustrated chronicle of dinosaur research, 1820's to 1960. Achievements of Cope, Marsh, Brown, Buckland, Mantell, Huxley, many others. 384pp. 5¼ × 8¼. 24701-5 Pa. $7.95

THE TASTEMAKERS, Russell Lynes. Informal, illustrated social history of American taste 1850's–1950's. First popularized categories Highbrow, Lowbrow, Middlebrow. 129 illustrations. New (1979) afterword. 384pp. 6 × 9. 23993-4 Pa. $8.95

DOUBLE CROSS PURPOSES, Ronald A. Knox. A treasure hunt in the Scottish Highlands, an old map, unidentified corpse, surprise discoveries keep reader guessing in this cleverly intricate tale of financial skullduggery. 2 black-and-white maps. 320pp. 5⅜ × 8½. (Available in U.S. only) 25032-6 Pa. $6.95

AUTHENTIC VICTORIAN DECORATION AND ORNAMENTATION IN FULL COLOR: 46 Plates from "Studies in Design," Christopher Dresser. Superb full-color lithographs reproduced from rare original portfolio of a major Victorian designer. 48pp. 9¼ × 12¼. 25083-0 Pa. $7.95

PRIMITIVE ART, Franz Boas. Remains the best text ever prepared on subject, thoroughly discussing Indian, African, Asian, Australian, and, especially, Northern American primitive art. Over 950 illustrations show ceramics, masks, totem poles, weapons, textiles, paintings, much more. 376pp. 5⅜ × 8. 20025-6 Pa. $7.95

SIDELIGHTS ON RELATIVITY, Albert Einstein. Unabridged republication of two lectures delivered by the great physicist in 1920–21. *Ether and Relativity* and *Geometry and Experience.* Elegant ideas in non-mathematical form, accessible to intelligent layman. vi + 56pp. 5⅜ × 8½. 24511-X Pa. $2.95

THE WIT AND HUMOR OF OSCAR WILDE, edited by Alvin Redman. More than 1,000 ripostes, paradoxes, wisecracks: Work is the curse of the drinking classes, I can resist everything except temptation, etc. 258pp. 5⅜ × 8½. 20602-5 Pa. $4.95

ADVENTURES WITH A MICROSCOPE, Richard Headstrom. 59 adventures with clothing fibers, protozoa, ferns and lichens, roots and leaves, much more. 142 illustrations. 232pp. 5⅜ × 8½. 23471-1 Pa. $3.95

PLANTS OF THE BIBLE, Harold N. Moldenke and Alma L. Moldenke. Standard reference to all 230 plants mentioned in Scriptures. Latin name, biblical reference, uses, modern identity, much more. Unsurpassed encyclopedic resource for scholars, botanists, nature lovers, students of Bible. Bibliography. Indexes. 123 black-and-white illustrations. 384pp. 6 × 9. 25069-5 Pa. $8.95

FAMOUS AMERICAN WOMEN: A Biographical Dictionary from Colonial Times to the Present, Robert McHenry, ed. From Pocahontas to Rosa Parks, 1,035 distinguished American women documented in separate biographical entries. Accurate, up-to-date data, numerous categories, spans 400 years. Indices. 493pp. 6½ × 9¼. 24523-3 Pa. $10.95

THE FABULOUS INTERIORS OF THE GREAT OCEAN LINERS IN HISTORIC PHOTOGRAPHS, William H. Miller, Jr. Some 200 superb photographs capture exquisite interiors of world's great "floating palaces"—1890's to 1980's: *Titanic, Ile de France, Queen Elizabeth, United States, Europa*, more. Approx. 200 black-and-white photographs. Captions. Text. Introduction. 160pp. 8⅜ × 11¼. 24756-2 Pa. $9.95

THE GREAT LUXURY LINERS, 1927–1954: A Photographic Record, William H. Miller, Jr. Nostalgic tribute to heyday of ocean liners. 186 photos of Ile de France, Normandie, Leviathan, Queen Elizabeth, United States, many others. Interior and exterior views. Introduction. Captions. 160pp. 9 × 12. 24056-8 Pa. $10.95

A NATURAL HISTORY OF THE DUCKS, John Charles Phillips. Great landmark of ornithology offers complete detailed coverage of nearly 200 species and subspecies of ducks: gadwall, sheldrake, merganser, pintail, many more. 74 full-color plates, 102 black-and-white. Bibliography. Total of 1,920pp. 8⅜ × 11¼. 25141-1, 25142-X Cloth. Two-vol. set $100.00

THE SEAWEED HANDBOOK: An Illustrated Guide to Seaweeds from North Carolina to Canada, Thomas F. Lee. Concise reference covers 78 species. Scientific and common names, habitat, distribution, more. Finding keys for easy identification. 224pp. 5⅜ × 8½. 25215-9 Pa. $6.95

THE TEN BOOKS OF ARCHITECTURE: The 1755 Leoni Edition, Leon Battista Alberti. Rare classic helped introduce the glories of ancient architecture to the Renaissance. 68 black-and-white plates. 336pp. 8⅜ × 11¼. 25239-6 Pa. $14.95

MISS MACKENZIE, Anthony Trollope. Minor masterpieces by Victorian master unmasks many truths about life in 19th-century England. First inexpensive edition in years. 392pp. 5⅜ × 8½. 25201-9 Pa. $8.95

THE RIME OF THE ANCIENT MARINER, Gustave Doré, Samuel Taylor Coleridge. Dramatic engravings considered by many to be his greatest work. The terrifying space of the open sea, the storms and whirlpools of an unknown ocean, the ice of Antarctica, more—all rendered in a powerful, chilling manner. Full text. 38 plates. 77pp. 9¼ × 12. 22305-1 Pa. $4.95

THE EXPEDITIONS OF ZEBULON MONTGOMERY PIKE, Zebulon Montgomery Pike. Fascinating first-hand accounts (1805-6) of exploration of Mississippi River, Indian wars, capture by Spanish dragoons, much more. 1,088pp. 5⅜ × 8½. 25254-X, 25255-8 Pa. Two-vol. set $25.90

A CONCISE HISTORY OF PHOTOGRAPHY: Third Revised Edition, Helmut Gernsheim. Best one-volume history—camera obscura, photochemistry, daguerreotypes, evolution of cameras, film, more. Also artistic aspects—landscape, portraits, fine art, etc. 281 black-and-white photographs. 26 in color. 176pp. 8⅜ × 11¼. 25128-4 Pa. $13.95

THE DORÉ BIBLE ILLUSTRATIONS, Gustave Doré. 241 detailed plates from the Bible: the Creation scenes, Adam and Eve, Flood, Babylon, battle sequences, life of Jesus, etc. Each plate is accompanied by the verses from the King James version of the Bible. 241pp. 9 × 12. 23004-X Pa. $9.95

WANDERINGS IN WEST AFRICA, Richard F. Burton. Great Victorian scholar/adventurer's invaluable descriptions of African tribal rituals, fetishism, culture, art, much more. Fascinating 19th-century account. 624pp. 5⅜ × 8½. 26890-X Pa. $12.95

FLATLAND, E. A. Abbott. Intriguing and enormously popular science-fiction classic explores the complexities of trying to survive as a two-dimensional being in a three-dimensional world. Amusingly illustrated by the author. 16 illustrations. 103pp. 5⅜ × 8½. 20001-9 Pa. $2.50

THE HISTORY OF THE LEWIS AND CLARK EXPEDITION, Meriwether Lewis and William Clark, edited by Elliott Coues. Classic edition of Lewis and Clark's day-by-day journals that later became the basis for U.S. claims to Oregon and the West. Accurate and invaluable geographical, botanical, biological, meteorological and anthropological material. Total of 1,508pp. 5⅜ × 8½. 21268-8, 21269-6, 21270-X Pa. Three-vol. set $26.85

LANGUAGE, TRUTH AND LOGIC, Alfred J. Ayer. Famous, clear introduction to Vienna, Cambridge schools of Logical Positivism. Role of philosophy, elimination of metaphysics, nature of analysis, etc. 160pp. 5⅜ × 8½. (Available in U.S. and Canada only) 20010-8 Pa. $3.95

MATHEMATICS FOR THE NONMATHEMATICIAN, Morris Kline. Detailed, college-level treatment of mathematics in cultural and historical context, with numerous exercises. For liberal arts students. Preface. Recommended Reading Lists. Tables. Index. Numerous black-and-white figures. xvi + 641pp. 5⅜ × 8½. 24823-2 Pa. $11.95

HANDBOOK OF PICTORIAL SYMBOLS, Rudolph Modley. 3,250 signs and symbols, many systems in full; official or heavy commercial use. Arranged by subject. Most in Pictorial Archive series. 143pp. 8⅛ × 11. 23357-X Pa. $6.95

INCIDENTS OF TRAVEL IN YUCATAN, John L. Stephens. Classic (1843) exploration of jungles of Yucatan, looking for evidences of Maya civilization. Travel adventures, Mexican and Indian culture, etc. Total of 669pp. 5⅜ × 8½. 20926-1, 20927-X Pa., Two-vol. set $11.90

DEGAS: An Intimate Portrait, Ambroise Vollard. Charming, anecdotal memoir by famous art dealer of one of the greatest 19th-century French painters. 14 black-and-white illustrations. Introduction by Harold L. Van Doren. 96pp. 5⅜ × 8½.
25131-4 Pa. $4.95

PERSONAL NARRATIVE OF A PILGRIMAGE TO ALMANDINAH AND MECCAH, Richard Burton. Great travel classic by remarkably colorful personality. Burton, disguised as a Moroccan, visited sacred shrines of Islam, narrowly escaping death. 47 illustrations. 959pp. 5⅜ × 8½.   21217-3, 21218-1 Pa., Two-vol. set $19.90

PHRASE AND WORD ORIGINS, A. H. Holt. Entertaining, reliable, modern study of more than 1,200 colorful words, phrases, origins and histories. Much unexpected information. 254pp. 5⅜ × 8½.   20758-7 Pa. $5.95

THE RED THUMB MARK, R. Austin Freeman. In this first Dr. Thorndyke case, the great scientific detective draws fascinating conclusions from the nature of a single fingerprint. Exciting story, authentic science. 320pp. 5⅜ × 8½. (Available in U.S. only)   25210-8 Pa. $6.95

AN EGYPTIAN HIEROGLYPHIC DICTIONARY, E. A. Wallis Budge. Monumental work containing about 25,000 words or terms that occur in texts ranging from 3000 B.C. to 600 A.D. Each entry consists of a transliteration of the word, the word in hieroglyphs, and the meaning in English. 1,314pp. 6⅝ × 10.
23615-3, 23616-1 Pa., Two-vol. set $35.90

THE COMPLEAT STRATEGYST: Being a Primer on the Theory of Games of Strategy, J. D. Williams. Highly entertaining classic describes, with many illustrated examples, how to select best strategies in conflict situations. Prefaces. Appendices. xvi + 268pp. 5⅜ × 8½.   25101-2 Pa. $6.95

THE ROAD TO OZ, L. Frank Baum. Dorothy meets the Shaggy Man, little Button-Bright and the Rainbow's beautiful daughter in this delightful trip to the magical Land of Oz. 272pp. 5⅜ × 8.   25208-6 Pa. $5.95

POINT AND LINE TO PLANE, Wassily Kandinsky. Seminal exposition of role of point, line, other elements in non-objective painting. Essential to understanding 20th-century art. 127 illustrations. 192pp. 6½ × 9¼.   23808-3 Pa. $5.95

LADY ANNA, Anthony Trollope. Moving chronicle of Countess Lovel's bitter struggle to win for herself and daughter Anna their rightful rank and fortune— perhaps at cost of sanity itself. 384pp. 5⅜ × 8½.   24669-8 Pa. $8.95

EGYPTIAN MAGIC, E. A. Wallis Budge. Sums up all that is known about magic in Ancient Egypt: the role of magic in controlling the gods, powerful amulets that warded off evil spirits, scarabs of immortality, use of wax images, formulas and spells, the secret name, much more. 253pp. 5⅜ × 8½.   22681-6 Pa. $4.50

THE DANCE OF SIVA, Ananda Coomaraswamy. Preeminent authority unfolds the vast metaphysic of India: the revelation of her art, conception of the universe, social organization, etc. 27 reproductions of art masterpieces. 192pp. 5⅜ × 8½.
24817-8 Pa. $5.95

CHRISTMAS CUSTOMS AND TRADITIONS, Clement A. Miles. Origin, evolution, significance of religious, secular practices. Caroling, gifts, yule logs, much more. Full, scholarly yet fascinating; non-sectarian. 400pp. 5⅜ × 8½.
23354-5 Pa. $6.95

THE HUMAN FIGURE IN MOTION, Eadweard Muybridge. More than 4,500 stopped-action photos, in action series, showing undraped men, women, children jumping, lying down, throwing, sitting, wrestling, carrying, etc. 390pp. 7⅞ × 10⅝.
20204-6 Cloth. $24.95

THE MAN WHO WAS THURSDAY, Gilbert Keith Chesterton. Witty, fast-paced novel about a club of anarchists in turn-of-the-century London. Brilliant social, religious, philosophical speculations. 128pp. 5⅜ × 8½.
25121-7 Pa. $3.95

A CEZANNE SKETCHBOOK: Figures, Portraits, Landscapes and Still Lifes, Paul Cezanne. Great artist experiments with tonal effects, light, mass, other qualities in over 100 drawings. A revealing view of developing master painter, precursor of Cubism. 102 black-and-white illustrations. 144pp. 8¾ × 6⅜.
24790-2 Pa. $6.95

AN ENCYCLOPEDIA OF BATTLES: Accounts of Over 1,560 Battles from 1479 B.C. to the Present, David Eggenberger. Presents essential details of every major battle in recorded history, from the first battle of Megiddo in 1479 B.C. to Grenada in 1984. List of Battle Maps. New Appendix covering the years 1967–1984. Index. 99 illustrations. 544pp. 6½ × 9¼.
24913-1 Pa. $14.95

AN ETYMOLOGICAL DICTIONARY OF MODERN ENGLISH, Ernest Weekley. Richest, fullest work, by foremost British lexicographer. Detailed word histories. Inexhaustible. Total of 856pp. 6½ × 9¼.
21873-2, 21874-0 Pa., Two-vol. set $19.90

WEBSTER'S AMERICAN MILITARY BIOGRAPHIES, edited by Robert McHenry. Over 1,000 figures who shaped 3 centuries of American military history. Detailed biographies of Nathan Hale, Douglas MacArthur, Mary Hallaren, others. Chronologies of engagements, more. Introduction. Addenda. 1,033 entries in alphabetical order. xi + 548pp. 6½ × 9¼. (Available in U.S. only)
24758-9 Pa. $13.95

LIFE IN ANCIENT EGYPT, Adolf Erman. Detailed older account, with much not in more recent books: domestic life, religion, magic, medicine, commerce, and whatever else needed for complete picture. Many illustrations. 597pp. 5⅜ × 8½.
22632-8 Pa. $8.95

HISTORIC COSTUME IN PICTURES, Braun & Schneider. Over 1,450 costumed figures shown, covering a wide variety of peoples: kings, emperors, nobles, priests, servants, soldiers, scholars, townsfolk, peasants, merchants, courtiers, cavaliers, and more. 256pp. 8⅜ × 11¼.
23150-X Pa. $9.95

THE NOTEBOOKS OF LEONARDO DA VINCI, edited by J. P. Richter. Extracts from manuscripts reveal great genius; on painting, sculpture, anatomy, sciences, geography, etc. Both Italian and English. 186 ms. pages reproduced, plus 500 additional drawings, including studies for *Last Supper, Sforza* monument, etc. 860pp. 7⅞ × 10¾. (Available in U.S. only) 22572-0, 22573-9 Pa., Two-vol. set $31.90

CATALOG OF DOVER BOOKS

THE ART NOUVEAU STYLE BOOK OF ALPHONSE MUCHA: All 72 Plates from "Documents Decoratifs" in Original Color, Alphonse Mucha. Rare copyright-free design portfolio by high priest of Art Nouveau. Jewelry, wallpaper, stained glass, furniture, figure studies, plant and animal motifs, etc. Only complete one-volume edition. 80pp. 9⅜ × 12¼. 24044-4 Pa. $9.95

ANIMALS: 1,419 COPYRIGHT-FREE ILLUSTRATIONS OF MAMMALS, BIRDS, FISH, INSECTS, ETC., edited by Jim Harter. Clear wood engravings present, in extremely lifelike poses, over 1,000 species of animals. One of the most extensive pictorial sourcebooks of its kind. Captions. Index. 284pp. 9 × 12.
23766-4 Pa. $9.95

OBELISTS FLY HIGH, C. Daly King. Masterpiece of American detective fiction, long out of print, involves murder on a 1935 transcontinental flight—"a very thrilling story"—NY Times. Unabridged and unaltered republication of the edition published by William Collins Sons & Co. Ltd., London, 1935. 288pp. 5⅜ × 8½. (Available in U.S. only) 25036-9 Pa. $5.95

VICTORIAN AND EDWARDIAN FASHION: A Photographic Survey, Alison Gernsheim. First fashion history completely illustrated by contemporary photographs. Full text plus 235 photos, 1840–1914, in which many celebrities appear. 240pp. 6½ × 9¼. 24205-6 Pa. $8.95

THE ART OF THE FRENCH ILLUSTRATED BOOK, 1700–1914, Gordon N. Ray. Over 630 superb book illustrations by Fragonard, Delacroix, Daumier, Doré, Grandville, Manet, Mucha, Steinlen, Toulouse-Lautrec and many others. Preface. Introduction. 633 halftones. Indices of artists, authors & titles, binders and provenances. Appendices. Bibliography. 608pp. 8⅜ × 11¼. 25086-5 Pa. $24.95

THE WONDERFUL WIZARD OF OZ, L. Frank Baum. Facsimile in full color of America's finest children's classic. 143 illustrations by W. W. Denslow. 267pp. 5⅜ × 8½. 20691-2 Pa. $7.95

FOLLOWING THE EQUATOR: A Journey Around the World, Mark Twain. Great writer's 1897 account of circumnavigating the globe by steamship. Ironic humor, keen observations, vivid and fascinating descriptions of exotic places. 197 illustrations. 720pp. 5⅜ × 8½. 26113-1 Pa. $15.95

THE FRIENDLY STARS, Martha Evans Martin & Donald Howard Menzel. Classic text marshalls the stars together in an engaging, non-technical survey, presenting them as sources of beauty in night sky. 23 illustrations. Foreword. 2 star charts. Index. 147pp. 5⅜ × 8½. 21099-5 Pa. $3.95

FADS AND FALLACIES IN THE NAME OF SCIENCE, Martin Gardner. Fair, witty appraisal of cranks, quacks, and quackeries of science and pseudoscience: hollow earth, Velikovsky, orgone energy, Dianetics, flying saucers, Bridey Murphy, food and medical fads, etc. Revised, expanded In the Name of Science. "A very able and even-tempered presentation."—The New Yorker. 363pp. 5⅜ × 8.
20394-8 Pa. $6.95

ANCIENT EGYPT: ITS CULTURE AND HISTORY, J. E Manchip White. From pre-dynastics through Ptolemies: society, history, political structure, religion, daily life, literature, cultural heritage. 48 plates. 217pp. 5⅜ × 8½. 22548-8 Pa. $5.95

SIR HARRY HOTSPUR OF HUMBLETHWAITE, Anthony Trollope. Incisive, unconventional psychological study of a conflict between a wealthy baronet, his idealistic daughter, and their scapegrace cousin. The 1870 novel in its first inexpensive edition in years. 250pp. 5⅜ × 8½. 24953-0 Pa. $6.95

LASERS AND HOLOGRAPHY, Winston E. Kock. Sound introduction to burgeoning field, expanded (1981) for second edition. Wave patterns, coherence, lasers, diffraction, zone plates, properties of holograms, recent advances. 84 illustrations. 160pp. 5⅜ × 8¼. (Except in United Kingdom) 24041-X Pa. $3.95

INTRODUCTION TO ARTIFICIAL INTELLIGENCE: SECOND, ENLARGED EDITION, Philip C. Jackson, Jr. Comprehensive survey of artificial intelligence—the study of how machines (computers) can be made to act intelligently. Includes introductory and advanced material. Extensive notes updating the main text. 132 black-and-white illustrations. 512pp. 5⅜ × 8½. 24864-X Pa. $8.95

HISTORY OF INDIAN AND INDONESIAN ART, Ananda K. Coomaraswamy. Over 400 illustrations illuminate classic study of Indian art from earliest Harappa finds to early 20th century. Provides philosophical, religious and social insights. 304pp. 6⅝ × 9⅝. 25005-9 Pa. $11.95

THE GOLEM, Gustav Meyrink. Most famous supernatural novel in modern European literature, set in Ghetto of Old Prague around 1890. Compelling story of mystical experiences, strange transformations, profound terror. 13 black-and-white illustrations. 224pp. 5⅜ × 8½. (Available in U.S. only) 25025-3 Pa. $6.95

PICTORIAL ENCYCLOPEDIA OF HISTORIC ARCHITECTURAL PLANS, DETAILS AND ELEMENTS: With 1,880 Line Drawings of Arches, Domes, Doorways, Facades, Gables, Windows, etc., John Theodore Haneman. Sourcebook of inspiration for architects, designers, others. Bibliography. Captions. 141pp. 9 × 12. 24605-1 Pa. $7.95

BENCHLEY LOST AND FOUND, Robert Benchley. Finest humor from early 30's, about pet peeves, child psychologists, post office and others. Mostly unavailable elsewhere. 73 illustrations by Peter Arno and others. 183pp. 5⅜ × 8½. 22410-4 Pa. $4.95

ERTÉ GRAPHICS, Erté. Collection of striking color graphics: *Seasons, Alphabet, Numerals, Aces* and *Precious Stones*. 50 plates, including 4 on covers. 48pp. 9⅜ × 12¼. 23580-7 Pa. $7.95

THE JOURNAL OF HENRY D. THOREAU, edited by Bradford Torrey, F. H. Allen. Complete reprinting of 14 volumes, 1837–61, over two million words; the sourcebooks for *Walden*, etc. Definitive. All original sketches, plus 75 photographs. 1,804pp. 8½ × 12¼. 20312-3, 20313-1 Cloth., Two-vol. set $125.00

CASTLES: THEIR CONSTRUCTION AND HISTORY, Sidney Toy. Traces castle development from ancient roots. Nearly 200 photographs and drawings illustrate moats, keeps, baileys, many other features. Caernarvon, Dover Castles, Hadrian's Wall, Tower of London, dozens more. 256pp. 5⅜ × 8¼. 24898-4 Pa. $6.95

CATALOG OF DOVER BOOKS

AMERICAN CLIPPER SHIPS: 1833–1858, Octavius T. Howe & Frederick C. Matthews. Fully-illustrated, encyclopedic review of 352 clipper ships from the period of America's greatest maritime supremacy. Introduction. 109 halftones. 5 black-and-white line illustrations. Index. Total of 928pp. 5⅜ × 8½.
25115-2, 25116-0 Pa., Two-vol. set $17.90

TOWARDS A NEW ARCHITECTURE, Le Corbusier. Pioneering manifesto by great architect, near legendary founder of "International School." Technical and aesthetic theories, views on industry, economics, relation of form to function, "mass-production spirit," much more. Profusely illustrated. Unabridged translation of 13th French edition. Introduction by Frederick Etchells. 320pp. 6⅛ × 9¼. (Available in U.S. only)
25023-7 Pa. $8.95

THE BOOK OF KELLS, edited by Blanche Cirker. Inexpensive collection of 32 full-color, full-page plates from the greatest illuminated manuscript of the Middle Ages, painstakingly reproduced from rare facsimile edition. Publisher's Note. Captions. 32pp. 9⅜ × 12¼.
24345-1 Pa. $4.95

BEST SCIENCE FICTION STORIES OF H. G. WELLS, H. G. Wells. Full novel *The Invisible Man*, plus 17 short stories: "The Crystal Egg," "Aepyornis Island," "The Strange Orchid," etc. 303pp. 5⅜ × 8½. (Available in U.S. only)
21531-8 Pa. $6.95

AMERICAN SAILING SHIPS: Their Plans and History, Charles G. Davis. Photos, construction details of schooners, frigates, clippers, other sailcraft of 18th to early 20th centuries—plus entertaining discourse on design, rigging, nautical lore, much more. 137 black-and-white illustrations. 240pp. 6⅛ × 9¼.
24658-2 Pa. $6.95

ENTERTAINING MATHEMATICAL PUZZLES, Martin Gardner. Selection of author's favorite conundrums involving arithmetic, money, speed, etc., with lively commentary. Complete solutions. 112pp. 5⅜ × 8½.
25211-6 Pa. $2.95

THE WILL TO BELIEVE, HUMAN IMMORTALITY, William James. Two books bound together. Effect of irrational on logical, and arguments for human immortality. 402pp. 5⅜ × 8½.
20291-7 Pa. $7.95

THE HAUNTED MONASTERY and THE CHINESE MAZE MURDERS, Robert Van Gulik. 2 full novels by Van Gulik continue adventures of Judge Dee and his companions. An evil Taoist monastery, seemingly supernatural events; overgrown topiary maze that hides strange crimes. Set in 7th-century China. 27 illustrations. 328pp. 5⅜ × 8½.
23502-5 Pa. $6.95

CELEBRATED CASES OF JUDGE DEE (DEE GOONG AN), translated by Robert Van Gulik. Authentic 18th-century Chinese detective novel; Dee and associates solve three interlocked cases. Led to Van Gulik's own stories with same characters. Extensive introduction. 9 illustrations. 237pp. 5⅜ × 8½.
23337-5 Pa. $5.95

Prices subject to change without notice.
Available at your book dealer or write for free catalog to Dept. GI, Dover Publications, Inc., 31 East 2nd St., Mineola, N.Y. 11501. Dover publishes more than 175 books each year on science, elementary and advanced mathematics, biology, music, art, literary history, social sciences and other areas.